For my mother, who had great legs once upon a time

I wish to acknowledge the traditional owners of this land on which I write and where most of these stories take place, the Wurundjeri people of the Kulin nation, as well as the traditional owners of the other areas mentioned in this book: the Boonwurrung people and Wadawurrung people of the Kulin nation, the Gunaikurnai people, the Kaurna people, the Antakirinja Matu-Yankunytjatjara people, the Larrakia people, and the Gadigal people of the Eora nation. I would like to also pay my respects to their Elders, past, present and future. First Nations people have cared for this land for more than 60,000 years, and sovereignty was never ceded.

Praise for *Sad Mum Lady*

'If David Sedaris and Sheila Heti had a baby ... well, there's a lot to unpack there. But the ensuing stories would be brutal and hilarious and endlessly readable. And they'd look a bit like *Sad Mum Lady*.'
—Michael Williams

'Hilarious and heartbreaking. Ashe Davenport captures the complexity of motherhood with astonishing humour, candour and humanity.'
—Georgie Dent

'Funny and sad, wise and vulnerable: Ashe Davenport's memoir of motherhood rang truer for me than any other book on the subject, perhaps including my own.'
—Lauren Sams

'The essays in this collection are unashamed, affording the same candour to the realities of motherhood on both the flesh and the mind. Any resistance the reader might feel to reading about mucus plugs or maternal rage is dismantled by Davenport's natural humour.'
—*The Age*

'Ashe Davenport's debut was a brilliant read that transcended any idea of genre or the narrow relevance of one's own experience. First and foremost it's a sharp, funny, frequently moving book of essays from a serious new writer.' —*The Guardian*

‘[*Sad Mum Lady*] is the opposite to the industry-generated manuals, shopping lists and official advice that can make new parents feel so helpless.’ —*Canberra Times*

‘A drily funny portrait of life after children.’ —*New Idea*

‘The antidote to yummy mummy culture . . . hilarious, honest and deeply relatable reading.’ —*Monde*

SAD MUM LADY

Ashe Davenport

ALLEN & UNWIN
SYDNEY • MELBOURNE • AUCKLAND • LONDON

This edition published 2022
First published in 2020

Certain names and details have been changed to protect the innocent and guilty alike.

Allen & Unwin
83 Alexander Street
Crows Nest NSW 2065
Australia
Phone: (61 2) 8425 0100
Email: info@allenandunwin.com
Web: www.allenandunwin.com

A catalogue record for this book is available from the National Library of Australia

ISBN 978 1 76106 733 4

Internal design by Midland Typesetters, Australia
Set in Bembo by Midland Typesetters, Australia
Printed in Australia by McPherson's Printing Group

10 9 8 7 6 5 4 3 2 1

The paper in this book is FSC® certified. FSC® promotes environmentally responsible, socially beneficial and economically viable management of the world's forests.

CONTENTS

AUTHOR'S NOTE

The first thing you need to know is that my family is at capacity on the name 'Sam'. It is my husband's name, my sister's name and my grandfather's name. They are three of my all-time favourite people, but I regretfully inform any adopters of this most solid appellation that we are not taking on anymore Sams at this time.

I have three sisters; Sam, as mentioned, Georgie and Parris. Our mother raised us with the efficiency and bloody-mindedness of a woman scorned, except for every other weekend, which we spent with our father, his wife and our half-brothers Jude and Tex.

My children's names are Franny and Dee Dee. At the time of writing they're aged two and three, just the right size to rest their heads on my chest when I read to them, the three of us breathing like leaves on a branch.

At times I've found parenthood harrowing, at others excruciating, however, this book is not a longwinded case for it being 'hard, but worth it'. It's a collection of stories told from the perspective of a privileged, selfish, occasionally well-meaning, angry depressive who snores like a pig and says funny things sometimes. My hope is that it will help some lonely people feel less alone.

THE MOTHERBOY UPSTAIRS

My upstairs neighbour and I were home a lot, me being 40 weeks pregnant and Tom a reclusive drug addict. We kept similar hours, sleeping most of the day and shuffling to and from the toilet of a night-time. He shared the apartment with his mother Vivienne, a 70-something ex-private school board member with a shimmering silver up-do. After the divorce, Vivienne sold her florist business and bought the place because of its proximity to the city. She figured her retirement as a sophisticated single woman would be best spent enjoying Melbourne's art and food scene, and hadn't planned on her 40-year-old son moving home to burst her bubble with an ice shard.

In the years before Tom's arrival, Sam and I had happily co-existed with Vivienne. Our duplex featured stained-glass windows, a sun-drenched courtyard and cheap rent, thanks to a benevolent landlord who had retired to her country home. We knew the milk bar owners' kids' names and had been on the waitlist for the local daycare centre for a year. It was the perfect place to start our parenting journey.

Vivienne got a job as a receptionist so she could financially support her troubled son. In return, Tom invited strangers into her living room for three-day drug benders when she was down the coast. Given our apartment was one of two, there was little mystery as to where the smell of burning chemicals or the sound of drum and bass was coming from. To get to the party, Tom's guests would first have to get past me, the pregnant troll in the stairwell assuming a wide-legged power stance and interrogating them about their life choices.

'Do you realise you're about to enter an elderly woman's home without her consent?' I'd ask, turning to profile so my belly could serve as a physical obstacle as well as an emotional one. 'Is that a choice you're comfortable with? How dare you squeeze past me like that. If you keep me awake I will GOBBLE YOU UP!'

I managed to quash a few of the parties, but the feeling of satisfaction was fleeting. Tom would fall behind on the money he owed drug dealers, and shaky demanding strangers would appear outside our building for weeks afterwards. Some scrawled letters and taped them to the security gate. Others attempted to break into the upstairs apartment via my outdoor setting in the courtyard.

Tom refused to answer the door to anyone, especially me. He ignored my passive aggressive notes and aggressive aggressive Facebook friend requests. I tried accosting Vivienne on bin night, to which she responded by explaining her son could have as many *guests* round as he liked, as if he were hosting a book club, while above us on the balcony her urine-soaked couch cushions aired their grievances.

When the pregnancy clock struck 41 weeks, I switched my phone off to avoid the increasingly frequent calls and texts asking if I'd 'had that baby yet?!' Sam became my sole contact with the outside world and my mother's only news source. I'd removed her contact privileges after she texted me a four-leaf clover emoji on what she had decided was my due date. It wasn't the date on my file at the hospital, but rather the one my mother had devised from her own calculations and marked in her diary as the day she would welcome her first grandchild. She'd asked to be in the delivery room and I hadn't had the heart to say no—that is, until I received the fateful clover.

'How is that helpful in any way?' I seethed into the phone, pacing the nature strip.

'Oh, you're being ridiculous,' she said. 'It was a bit of fun!'

The next-door neighbour turned off her hose and inspected the roses near the fence.

'I don't want you there during the birth. You never even asked me. It's not what I want.'

'You're just saying that to hurt me,' she said.

'It's not about you! Hi, Carole ... No, still no baby ... Yep, planning on a vaginal birth, thanks for asking ... Mum, are you there? Mum?'

Sam was my birth partner, PR manager and pizza delivery boy all rolled into one, but unfortunately he also had a job he was required to be at Monday to Friday, which left me alone with my thoughts. The hours meandered by. I passed the time packing and repacking my hospital bag, staring from the doorway of the quiet nursery and obsessing over Tom. The art deco era may have blessed our building with stained-glass window features, but it also meant shit was old. The ceiling creaked and groaned with every move Tom made and my neck and shoulders tightened accordingly. Each creak was a reminder that his next bender was just around the corner, and that life as a parent was going to be frustrating and unpredictable thanks solely to Tom. A healthy response might have been to step away from the neutral-toned onesies and go for a walk, but instead I sank deeper into the couch under the groaning ceiling, dreaming of scenarios that would lead to Tom moving out.

I imagined coming home to discover him lying in the stairwell, breathing shallowly, having fallen down the stairs on his way to the shops. I'd cradle his head in my lap while we waited for the ambulance, the frailness of his injured body suddenly revealing the fragility of his soul. His pain would flash before my eyes in vivid detail—his absent father, perhaps some vicious bullying he endured at the notoriously toxic boys' school of which his mother was on the board, his lack of self-belief, his loneliness, his drug use being the only way he knew how to feel like he belonged, if only for a moment. My tears would rain down on him in a water birth of my higher self. Due to the spinal injury, Tom would move to a long-term rehab centre where he would fall in love with his physiotherapist, with whom he would eventually move to a remote island off the coast of New Zealand. Despite Vivienne's joy over her son's newfound happiness, his absence would leave a void in her life, which she would fill by babysitting my child any time of the day or night.

I awoke one afternoon from such a reverie to the sound of Tom's doorbell. I was 40-weeks plus ten days, or 'preg af', as I believe it is referred to in the medical profession. I rolled off the couch into a kneeling position and waited, listening for any movements upstairs like a barn owl locating its prey. There was a single creak, then nothing. I heaved myself into a standing position and padded down the hallway to the nursery, the window of which looked out onto the security entrance. Standing at the gate was the same woman who had rung Tom's doorbell several times that week. She looked young and far from home.

'Tom!' she yelled. 'Open the door, please!'

I gathered she'd left something behind and was trying to get it back. Tom and Vivienne had been home during each of her previous attempts to do so, and hadn't come to the door. The cast-iron doorbells in our building could be heard from a block away, so it's safe to say this was no accident. Seeing the lights on upstairs, the young woman had grown more frustrated with each visit and had taken to pressing on the bell for minutes at a time. It was loud from our apartment, but upstairs it must have been face-melting. I imagined Tom hiding under the doona of his childhood bed while Vivienne banged dishes around the kitchen sink, humming maniacally until the girl called it quits for the night.

'Please!' she said, crying now. 'I just need my keys! I can't get into my accommodation!'

I imagined her bag stuffed deep under Tom's

bed, having taken on the significance of the telltale heart.

'Just throw my keys in the laneway and you'll never see me again!' she persisted.

My heart went out to her. Also, I felt that I could leverage her situation to achieve the Ultimate Goal of getting Tom evicted, and so I went to the gate to meet her.

'He's home, just so you know,' I said, leaning heavily against the wheelie bin inside the security entrance. 'I can hear him scurrying around up there. I live in the apartment downstairs. Are you okay?'

'Sorry about the noise,' she said, her eyes widening briefly at the size of my belly. 'I'm Hannah. Tom has my bag. I'm just trying to get it back.'

'You poor thing,' I said. 'Can I make you a cup of tea? The kettle's just boiled.'

'Um, okay.'

I led the way down the hall and suggested to Hannah that she call the police.

'Wow, do you think?' she asked, as we walked into the living room. She perched on the edge of the couch and I went to make the tea.

'At this point it's theft,' I called from the kitchen, cheerfully opening a packet of biscuits. 'He's committed a criminal act that's rendered you homeless! You can use my phone.'

I returned and placed the tea and biscuits on the coffee table, just out of reach, and handed Hannah my phone. After years of fielding my complaints about Tom, surely the police would jump at the opportunity to finally pin something on him. I could already see the cars arriving to make his arrest, starting with hostage-style negotiations from the street with a megaphone before opening his door by force. Handcuffed, Tom would be led to the back of one of the cars in disgrace. With her bag safely returned, Hannah would hug me and whisper, 'My angel,' before disappearing into the night. Tom's prison sentence would leave a void in Vivienne's life, which she'd fill by babysitting my child any time of the day or night.

Three hours later there was still no sign of the police. Hannah was muttering to herself and pacing the hallway. I was playing Candy Crush in the living room, having lost interest in the saga some time earlier.

A jangle of keys at the security gate echoed in the stairwell.

'The mum's home!' I yelled to Hannah. 'Her name's Vivienne! Go talk to her!'

Hannah ran to meet her, leaving the front door open. I curled up to the sound of their confrontation.

'*My* Tom has *your* handbag? Am I hearing that correctly?' Vivienne said in her fanciest voice. 'Tom is away at the moment, darling. Who's the designer? I can certainly have a look for it.'

'Sportsgirl,' replied Hannah. 'That'd be great, thanks!'

I was impressed by Hannah's improv skills. She'd dove into the scene without missing a beat. In it, Vivienne was a mother hearing about a girl's handbag for the first time. And Tom wasn't upstairs clinging to the back of his bedroom door pretending to be a dressing-gown.

Vivienne returned seconds later with the bag.

'Is this yours, darling?' she asked.

Hannah shrieked like a contestant on *The Price is Right*. 'Yes! That's it! Thank you so much!'

Vivienne told her she was more than welcome and wished the charming new member of her son's book club a fabulous evening. I heard her ascend the stairs and the click of her front door as she closed herself in with her love.

GET THE HOSE

If you slept over at my house during the nineties, I can almost guarantee that you saw my mother's vagina. She slept in the nude and had little patience for late-night noise. So little, in fact, that she couldn't spare half a second to throw on a dressing-gown before appearing in the doorway to unleash her wrath. If my friends and I were lucky, she'd fire a warning shot from her bedroom at the other end of our suburban home—either 'ENOUGH!' or a simple guttural scream—but more often than not she preferred to skip the pleasantries. The house shook as she stomped through the living room, sending us screaming back to our beds. When she burst through the door, mid naked tirade, it was like something out of a horror movie. A good one. As iconic as an axe through a bathroom door or a bucket of pig's blood. Such fear did her furious bush strike in the hearts of my guests that few dared to return, and the myth of my mother the nudist banshee swirled through the schoolyard. That may have had very little to do with her yelling without clothes on. 'Nudist banshee' was probably one of the friendlier terms for a single mother at the time.

In rare moments of respite between working, cooking, cleaning or coaching one of an infinite number of junior netball teams, my mother would sunbake in the backyard wearing only a visor. She enjoyed an all-over tan, unencumbered by the lines left by bathing suits. If my sisters or I brought a friend outside, she might reach languidly for a towel, but more often than not she would remain splayed on the deck, having fallen asleep in the sun.

When my mother did dress it was with understated style. She didn't like to stand out from the crowd. At university, she completed a coveted textiles degree, which informed her wardrobe of clean lines and impeccable tailoring. Her clothing was functional and pleasing to the eye. Outside of a torn Eurythmics singlet she sometimes wore around the house, she didn't use it to convey anything particularly personal.

For all her knowledge of and passion for fabric, she felt most like herself without a stitch of it.

The fights in our house were loud and often naked, due to most of them being over who stole what item of clothing. No insult was off limits and no bedroom door was un-slammed. My mother would threaten to remove the doors and occasionally followed through with the screwdriver. At various stages our bedrooms featured beach towels gaffer-taped to door frames.

The teenage era brought further turmoil. There were scorned exes, friend dramas and sinister older boyfriends bearing bouquets of STDs. I once watched aghast from the kitchen as my mother hosed one of mine down the driveway, like he was a pile of leaves. She'd been watering the garden when he arrived, wearing her signature visor and the bikini she reserved for front yard duties. Kostas was four years older than me and heir to a chain of strip clubs. He'd arrived with the intention of pressuring me into sex on a secluded part of the beach, and had figured my mother to be a minor obstacle in the proceedings.

'Hi, Mrs Davenport,' he said. 'I'm here to pick up your daughter.'

'Not in those clothes, I hope,' replied my mother, playfully spraying his t-shirt with water.

Kostas laughed and feigned horror. He was used to older women flirting with him.

'You'd better go home and change,' she said, increasing the water pressure and adjusting her aim to Kostas' eyes.

Kostas screamed as he stumbled blindly down the driveway, tripping backwards onto the footpath and springing up so suddenly that he slipped again in the rapids. He sat hugging his knees, red-eyed and drenched as my mother calmly closed the gate and returned to her gardening.

My mother's body was her armour, her safe place, where she kept my sisters and me for 36 months, our trust in life developing undisturbed. My father left her when we were aged zero to six for a 21-year-old with long blonde hair. One night, not long after it happened, my mother sat on the kitchen floor, the four of us screaming and grabbing at her, looking up at a can of baked beans on the counter and willing herself to stand so she could open it. *No one is going to open that can except me*, she repeated to herself, hopelessly at first, then factually, again and again until she could muster the strength to stand. My mother's body kept her heart beating after it broke. She draped it across the decking and planted it in the front yard, hand on hip, hose at the ready.

Other men came into her life. One moved into the house next door and coached kids' netball teams, like her. He had a daughter who fit perfectly in the middle of us. He loved my mother and she loved him. He wanted more children and she did not. He left her for a younger, softer woman who did.

By the time Georgie and I moved out, my mother was spending her evenings behind a closed door in the front room. She ate her meals in there and drank large glasses of wine, watching what she liked on her own television. Sam and Parris were high school students who knew how to put on a load of washing, make a stir-fry and organise their own lift to netball. She still coached a team or two, but the job had become tense and political. Her social world shrunk to the occasional drink with another beleaguered member of the netball community. Outside of making the odd school formal dress, my mother rarely used her textiles degree. Over the years, she worked as the payroll person for various companies in the retail sector. When the last of her children had moved out, she cloaked her armour in a terry cloth dressing-gown and braced herself for a long winter.

'Why would you want to live so far away from us?' I asked her years later, pregnant for the second time.

She'd sold our family home and bought a place an hour and a half out of town.

'I like my new job,' said my mother. 'And the golf courses.'

We were on our way to see Patti Smith perform *Horses* at Hamer Hall. The event had sold out in minutes, but my mother secured tickets through some new golfing buddies who were unable to attend. She wore elegant silver earrings and glasses with bright orange frames. Patti wore an oversized men's suit like it was a ball gown and spat on the stage. We danced in the aisle to 'Because the Night', during which I peed my pants a little bit Because the Pregnancy, and the happiness.

My mother timed her move wisely, as in the space of three years she became a grandmother five times over. She welcomed the onslaught of children with open arms, but from enough of a distance to be able to babysit on her terms. When she offered to take my kids for a sleepover, I jumped at the opportunity, and drove the 2.5 renditions of the *Moana* soundtrack to get there.

She'd made some changes to the place since I'd seen it last, getting rid of the carpet and extending the height of her backyard fence.

'You're not still sunbaking, are you?' I said, from one of her carefully selected kitchen stools. 'Please tell me you've discovered sunscreen.'

'No, I just wanted a bit more privacy out there. In case I'm having breakfast and need a sprig of parsley.'

'Naked,' I said.

'If it's warm enough.'

That night I went out for dinner with Sam. Parenthood had dulled our once-sparkling conversation, and made us more sensitive and generally paranoid due to the exhaustion, but we held hands when we walked back to the car, a small part of us still believing we'd make it through. My mother sent a video of the kids jumping in tutus on her bed, squealing and loopy with joy.

Me: *Looks like a fever dream. Were they ok today?*

Mum: *Angels. Though they saw me go Crocodile Dundee on the neighbour. He came flying up the driveway about the sprinkler again.*

Me: *Did you get him with the hose?*

Mum: *Not quite.*

I'd been following her saga with her new neighbour for some time. Her front sprinkler flooded his garage, and my mother got tired of waiting for him to install a retaining wall and had gone back to using it. He chastised her at her door on several occasions after dark. My mother assured me her neighbour's timing was tactical, designed to achieve optimal intimidation.

'It's what they do,' she explained the next day when I came to pick up the kids, 'when there isn't another man around.'

I recalled the neighbour who used to live across the street who would bang on our front door, furious over my sister's car blocking a centimetre of his driveway, and Mum facing the barrage in her dressing-gown, always late at night.

'He wasn't expecting to see two small children in tutus,' she said, laughing. 'He got quite the shock.'

Toys and colouring books lay strewn across her newly polished floorboards. On the wall was the large-scale print of Van Gogh's *Sunflowers* that used to hang in the kitchen of our childhood home, its glass broken and repaired several times from flying dishes and Nokia 52s. The sliding door to her courtyard was open, the sun on it revealing a mosaic of saliva and handprints.

'He sounds disgusting,' said Sam, a look on his face like he'd walked into a fart. 'Want me to go and talk to him?'

'I don't think we'll be seeing him anytime soon,' said my mother, sucking something from between her front teeth, perhaps a piece of her neighbour's liver.

'Did the kids fight?' I asked.

'There was a bit of argy-bargy over the unicorn,' she said. 'I'll have to get two of the fuckers.'

My mother waved us off from the driveway of the unit she owned in full, her queendom, where her garden would bloom without apology, and no man would enter unless expressly invited. She told me once that the role of a parent was 'a short-term caretaker' and I said it was the bleakest thing I'd ever heard. She said it wasn't bleak at all, because it meant we were on separate pathways that intertwined, and we got to be in each other's lives because we wanted to be. At last she felt the sun on her skin again, as she travelled along, parsley sprig in hand.

24 HOUR PARTUM PEOPLE

It was 5.30 a.m. when we got to the hospital. Sam parked the car and we sat for a while listening to some pan flute by a babbling brook, track three of my labour playlist, which I'd anxiously crafted to encourage the stress-free birth of our first child. He turned off the engine.

'Ready?' he asked.

'Nope,' I replied.

'More flute?'

'Go on.'

At 42 weeks, I'd succumbed to the hospital's insistence that I have my labour induced. I was fine, the baby was fine, but there were increased risks the longer

I was pregnant. At my last appointment, an obstetrician I'd never met put a cold hand on my belly and said if I didn't get induced I risked my baby being stillborn. He had a lazy eye and I was unsure whether he was talking to me or the med student taking notes in the corner. (Later that evening, at the bottom of an internet rabbit hole, I discovered that the risk of stillbirth had been surprisingly high throughout all stages of my pregnancy, and found that oddly reassuring.) There were risks associated with induction, too, but they were the kind that could be monitored by the hospital, the obstetrician explained. There may have been no risks had I waited for spontaneous labour, but nobody could say for sure.

Friends, the internet and strangers on the bus bombarded me with techniques to shake my baby loose. I tried acupuncture, spicy curry, raspberry leaf tea, walking, squatting, bouncing, rocking and having more sex than a Mykonos DJ, but nothing worked. I was extremely tense over not going into spontaneous labour, which was the antithesis of what I needed to feel to go into spontaneous labour. There may have also been some hoarse whisperings from the bowels of my soul telling me I was going to be a terrible mother and my body needed to protect my daughter from me for as long as possible. Either way, there's such a thing as too much tikka masala.

After some more pan flute, followed by three minutes of rain on a tent, Sam and I walked slowly to the entrance. Inside the waiting room were my fellow inductees: three women with their partners and one on her own. She was chatting to the nurse at reception while resting her elbows on the counter and rocking her hips from side to side. Her hair fell loose about her shoulders and on her feet she wore a pair of green thongs printed with pineapples. She seemed completely at ease. Her seventh kid, perhaps, or just a far more sensible relationship with herself and the world around her than I could ever hope to achieve.

A woman with a clipboard appeared in the doorway to summon us for our first round of 'cervical ripening', which is one of those medical terms that almost certainly was invented by a horny vampire during the sixteenth century, along with 'bone flap', 'drainage tube' and 'creeping eruption'. Once in the clinic upstairs, we peeled off into beds partitioned by pale blue curtains. Sam and I were joined by Judy the midwife, whose surname, if I had to guess, would be 'Holiday' or 'Gallop', or something equally brimming with hope. She made me feel relaxed, which was impressive considering she was a perfect stranger who was fingering my cervix at 6 a.m.

'I'm just disturbing these membranes,' she said sunnily, wrist deep. 'You're doing really well, Ashe.'

She wasn't wrong—I hadn't run scream-crying out of the building once—but the day was young.

Membranes sufficiently disturbed, we headed to the food court for breakfast. Since I was officially in medically induced labour, we'd been advised to stay on hospital grounds in case anything changed, like passengers of a delayed flight at an airport. We surveyed the display of sweating, pre-toasted sandwiches and decided to take our business to a nearby cafe. It was only a couple of blocks away and had great reviews. Besides, the walk would do me good.

It was 8 a.m. and already 31 degrees outside, day five of a six-day heatwave in an unsettlingly warm March. A hot gust of wind whipped my hair against my face. I leaned heavily on Sam at the pedestrian crossing as a weird, synthetic cramp tugged at my groin.

'Do you think they'll have a BLT?' I asked.

'I'd assume so,' said Sam. 'If I have to hogtie the chef and make you one myself, that's what I'll do.'

'Deal.'

We arrived at the bustling cafe and were greeted by a tall, slim youth with a silver cross dangling from his earlobe.

'Two of you, babe? It's going to be a twenty-minute wait.'

'No worries,' I said, resting a hand on my belly.

'There might be three of us by then, but I'll let you know if I start crowning.'

He nodded. 'A table for three will be closer to half an hour.'

'Two will be fine,' said Sam. 'We're due back at the hospital very soon, so if there's anything you can do to speed things up that would be great.'

I wondered what a gal had to do to get a table at a cafe in this town, because apparently being in labour didn't cut it. I stood with my legs apart and both hands on my lower back, a pregnancy power stance that, if coupled with an unblinking stare into a maître d's skinny soul, will soon get you a table by the window and an apology in the form of a complimentary smoothie.

The noise of the cafe and the sun through the window pane made my head spin. I ordered a BLT and excused myself to the toilet, where inside the cubicle I pressed my forehead against the cool metal door and drafted my online review:

Contracting Cathy! *Great coffee but disappointing labour facilities. Consider a birthing ball in the restroom or a dash of morphine in the Berry Bonanza.*

A drop of sweat rolled down the side of my face. There was a knock on the door, followed by an unfamiliar voice: 'Hi, um, your friend just asked me to check on you?'

'Oh! Ha! I'm fine!' I replied, flushing the toilet to demonstrate the fact. 'I'll be out in just a sec.'

I'd been gone for a while; long enough for our food to arrive. I confessed to Sam that I was feeling pretty out of it and we got our food to go. We sat in pools of sweat in an un-air-conditioned taxi back to the hospital. The BLT travelled well.

While I waited in a booth in the food court, Sam went to get us cups of tea. A kid with their grandparents walked shyly past me. They were carrying a new teddy and beaming into the floor, on their way to a very important meeting.

'It's Earl Grey,' said Sam apologetically. 'I tried two places, no English breakfast! Can you believe it?'

'That's insane,' I replied, looking properly at his face for the first time that day. 'How are you going with all of this?'

'Who, me?' he asked, taking a second to place himself. 'I'm okay, I think. Excited. A bit guilty and useless. Proud of you, mostly.'

'Already? All I've done is eat breakfast and get a cramp.' We kissed, and I remembered that I'd also made a central nervous system out of a drop of semen, and an entire human was about to burst through my body like a showgirl out of a cake. You're welcome, I thought, brushing an eyelash from his cheek. And I forgive you.

★

By the afternoon my labour pains had become too big a spectacle to browse the hospital gift shop, but not big enough to qualify me for a birthing suite. We set up camp on a vinyl couch by the lift in the lobby, on which I lay on my side groaning like an adult walrus. At my last cervical examination Judy had reported that I was two centimetres dilated. I almost slapped her when she told me. If labour was like climbing Mount Everest, two centimetres isn't even base camp one. It's the car hire place back in Tibet. Ordinarily, if a labouring woman turns up to the hospital when she's two centimetres dilated she's given a Panadol and sent home by the midwives, their laughter echoing down the corridor as she waddles back to her car in disgrace. As an inductee, going home wasn't an option. I'd signed a contract that morning before boarding the induction train. The hospital owned my whereabouts and mortal soul.

My grandmother rode her bike to the hospital for her first and third births. She almost had her second on the floor of the women's department at Myer Emporium. She put herself on a tram for that one, her one-year-old on her hip.

'I popped them out like peas!' she told me on a number of occasions during my pregnancy.

My mother needed little more than a cool wash-cloth to aid her in the births of my sisters and me.

She had active births, every one of them, and never set foot in a stirrup, I'd best believe. She stayed in the hospital for a week after each, but she would have been deemed fit enough to go home the same day, if that was what they did then, which it wasn't. There was a lot more care for new mothers in those days, she'd have me know.

Secretly, I'd hoped to be the woman who sneezed out her baby in the back of her taxi en route to the hospital, citing positive affirmations as the reason for her swift and uncomplicated birth. The cleaning bill wouldn't be cheap, of course, but we'd have forged a lifelong friendship with the driver, which some might consider to be priceless. Martin would attend our child's birthday party every year without fail. It would be nothing really, just a small gesture of our deep and profound connection with someone whose name we would otherwise never have remembered. It would just be a quaint little tradition of ours.

I'd been advised to expose myself exclusively to positive birth stories during pregnancy, but the books and people doing the advising failed to mention one key piece of information: positive birth story tellers were, for the most part, insufferable brags.

'Mum?' I was lying on a bed in a corridor outside the delivery ward, unsure if I was hallucinating my mother standing at my bedside.

'I'm not staying,' she said. 'I just wanted to give you this and wish you luck.'

It was a colouring book for adults, claiming to 'quiet the chaotic mind'. There were pencils, too. It was to help me pass the time, she explained, and 'get in the zone'. It might have annoyed me had I not been so glad to see her.

She kissed my forehead.

'I'm not sniffing around for an invitation,' she said.

'I know, Mum. I love you.'

'Darl, they're getting a room ready for you, just hang in there,' came a voice from above.

It was Judy. She wore a casual jacket and her handbag dangled from her shoulder. A final good deed for the long day. Angels walk among us and her name is Judy, I tried to express, mutely gripping her arm.

The birthing suite was significantly bigger than my living room, featuring a private ensuite and large window with a view of the city. It was 5 p.m. and the sky was thick and grey. The trees flung back and forth in the wind like they were advertising a car wash. Heavy clouds bulged around the tops of the buildings in the distance.

'Everything's looking good, Ashe,' said Kristy, my new midwife, a dry, capable sort, 'but things are at a bit of a standstill. I'd suggest moving to the oxytocin drip.'

'Can we wait a little bit longer?' I asked through the side of my gas mask.

'That's not really an option, unfortunately,' she said.

'I'm not doing that without an epidural.'

'Do you want to just see how you go first?'

'No, but thank you.'

The anaesthetist arrived shortly afterwards. She entered seated on a wheelie stool, propelling herself along with her feet either side of it, like a hairdresser scooting over to the cupboard for an extra comb. Her sheer confidence was reassuring. I sat on the edge of the bed while she prepped me for a local anaesthetic.

'No partners over this side, please,' she said, coolly marking up my spinal portal. 'We try to limit the number of patients in the birth suites to just the one.'

I figured partners who had fainted from seeing an epidural put in place were dispatched to a room down the hall, where the midwives would spend their breaks lazily drawing dicks on their faces.

It was after midnight, and Kristy suggested Sam take a nap on the hard square birthing mat in the corner. She offered no blanket or pillow, just the square, fit for a family dog. It wasn't that he was being punished, because that would imply he had some kind of significance in her mind. If I was a passenger in the birth, Sam was a tin can by the side of the road we'd burned past several towns ago. He knew his place, and accepted it gratefully. With a baby blanket covering a third of his torso, he fell asleep instantly.

My contractions raged while outside rain slapped silently against the triple-pane glass. My baby was in deep shit, but nobody knew it at the time. My labour was on autopilot and Kristy was seeing to other rooms. Stretched across my belly was the fetal heart monitor, its findings reflected in garish green on a small dark screen.

The numbers slowed then stumbled back towards the normal range. It was typical for a baby's heart rate to slow during a contraction, but I discovered later my induced contractions were triggering actual contractions. They were happening back to back. My baby wasn't getting enough time to breathe between the waves, like a surfer flung from her board and caught in a rip. This was one of the 'monitored risks' the obstetrician had spoken about, the kind favoured by the hospital over the hypothetical ones, but where were the people monitoring?

Boom

Boom

Boom

I remember light filling the room and Sam at my side, and the way the teddy bear blanket draped over one of his shoulders. I remember more and more people appearing: a paediatric surgeon, a neonatologist and various experts in bandanas of blue and green.

'We need to get this baby out, Ashe,' said an obstetrician. 'I'm going to give you an episiotomy then we're going to try a vacuum birth, okay?'

I remember the emptiness of my mind. 'Okay,' I said.

'Listen to me,' Kristy was saying, 'you need to push now, Ashe, really push.'

If you've ever wondered how to push a baby out when you can't feel your vagina, it's how I imagine Helen Keller learned the meaning of the word 'water': through common magic. Between that and the vacuum, my baby began to emerge. The hospital SWAT team glanced at their pagers and, one by one, excused themselves to more urgent matters.

Diana Day Mackenport was born at 5.30 a.m. on 18 March 2016. Her birth year would see the deaths of David Bowie, Prince, Carrie Fisher, Debbie Reynolds, Gene Wilder, George Michael, Leonard Cohen, Muhammad Ali, William Christopher, Alan Rickman and Harper Lee—an unfathomable funeral procession of people who inspired, changed and were beloved by the world, but not a single one more inspiring to me, more world-changing, more beloved.

RE: WE MISS YOU AT THE SALON!

Dear valued client,

It's been a while since we've seen you at the salon! Is there a specific reason for you not returning? If you were unhappy with something, we would love the opportunity to discuss it and make things right!

Warm regards,
The team at High Street Salon

Hi team,

Thanks for checking in. Four weeks ago I had a baby and my world has shrunk to a handful of rooms, which I travel between slowly, perched atop a maternity pad the size and weight of a beach towel. My body is a life factory and my brain is a pool of milk. When people say 'baby brain', what they mean is the most significant neurobiological transformation of a woman's adult life. The permanent structural changes to my brain triggered by pregnancy and motherhood have been passed down through the millennia and are designed to transform me into a fierce protector of my young. A haircut couldn't be further from my mind.

Also, I was a little disappointed by your reading selection last time. I was offered a newspaper and an old *Woman's Day* with hair clippings between the pages. It was disgusting, if I'm being completely honest. Who reads the news at the hairdressers?

My daughter is a way off requiring a trim. Currently she has seven hairs on her otherwise bald head. She looks like G.I. Jane and seems to possess a similar brand of steely determination. When she isn't feeding (always) or sleeping (rarely), she screams like a navy trainee on a gruelling obstacle course in the rain. She is outraged to be here and I don't blame her. Ten months ago, she was just minding her own business in non-existence when Sam and I plucked her from the abyss, gave her a human form and forced her hand on a contract that made her our property for the next eighteen years. We haven't got the faintest idea what we're doing either, which is rich. She lived in a house the size of a pear for almost a year and I couldn't sit through a two-minute tutorial on how to collapse her pram.

Really? said her screams, on my fifth and final attempt before shoving the unfolded contraption in the boot and driving off with the door open.

You've got to be kidding me, she cried, as I vomited over the side of the bath at the sight of her bellybutton floating by.

I imagine I would feel a similar level of disappointment had I moved to another planet and nothing was ready when I arrived—and the only person I could ask for help was a sleep-deprived greasy giant who didn't speak a lick of English.

'Greetings, giant lady!' I'd say, after an hour of floating around the abandoned half-built airport. 'Could I trouble you for a glass of Tang?'

'Glick glarck smarghft mnnnk,' she'd reply, binding my arms to my sides, gagging me with latex and confining me to a brightly coloured jail cell.

Alone in my hospital bed, I'd watched my newborn baby through the plastic side of her capsule, a mummified specimen from a far-off land. Her eyes were open and crossed deeply inwards, her mouth opening and closing like a goldfish in a bowl.

'Who sent you?' I whispered in the dark.

Never mind that, she tried her best to communicate. *Less talk, more Tang.*

A catheter bag wasn't in my birth plan. In the small hours of the morning, I awoke to a pulling sensation on my freshly stitched perineum. The bag was heavy with urine. A friendly midwife had emptied it for me sometime earlier, but she'd long since gone home. I rang for assistance and an unfamiliar woman appeared at my bedside.

'What is it?' she asked.

'Hi . . .' I squinted at her ID card in the dim light. 'Ruth. Um, my catheter bag's full?'

'In here,' Ruth replied, opening the door to the room's shared bathroom.

I stood up gingerly and moved slowly across the floor, clutching the bag by its tube to keep it from pulling on my stitches.

'There,' Ruth said, pointing to the toilet.

I looked down at my golden clutch and back at Ruth, blinking under the fluorescent lights.

'Hold it over the bowl and release the valve,' she said from the doorway, arms crossed.

I did as she said, trying to recall a moment in my life when I had felt more alone. If motherhood was a sorority this was the hazing stage, and Ruth was a stone-cold veteran sister who specialised in humiliation.

Task accomplished, I turned to Ruth, awaiting my next instruction.

'Wash your hands,' she said, and left.

Days after getting home from the hospital I was momentarily energised by a wave of oxytocin, and announced that I wanted to have breakfast at our local cafe as a family of three. By the time we got there, my energy levels had taken a turn for the worse. I'd slept for eight hours of the last 72. I couldn't have said for sure if I was dreaming or awake.

'You had the baby!' exclaimed the waitress. 'How was the birth?' she asked, in the casual way people sometimes do.

I looked up from my menu like a cow in a paddock at a passing car. 'Supes amaze,' I said, an expression I had never used prior to that moment nor haven't since.

'That's so cool,' she said. 'Let me tell you about the specials . . .'

I left the house again during week two. A young woman walked at my heels, unable to pass due to my pram and the freshly emptied bins that lined the footpath.

'Save yourself!' I said, pulling over the pram to let her by, surprised by my own choice of words and the way they rolled off my tongue.

She laughed uncomfortably and hurried to her appointment. A class maybe, or a day date, or a shift at a job she could quit at any moment. As I watched her full-bodied ponytail bounce into the distance I ran my fingers over my postpartum bald spot.

Out of interest, what do you have in the way of wigs? It would be nice not to always have to resort to the dog filter when I post Instagram stories about how well everything is going.

The insistence that I practise self-care is one of many paradoxes I have come across since becoming a parent. *Do something that's just for you*, the books say. *Slap on a face mask and take a candlelit bath, because you're worth it, Mama Bear. But also present your blood-blistered nipples to a tiny mouth with the suction power of a jet engine 24 hours a day, seven days a week you faceless, sleepless host organism.*

I couldn't bear to look at myself in those big mirrors for an extended period of time. I'd be looking at someone who looked vaguely like a person I thought I knew. I'd cry hysterically, or laugh, or both at the same time. It would be very alarming for the other patrons. That said, scheduling a hair appointment is a goal I didn't know I had until now, so thank you for the thoughtful prompt. No doubt you'll hear from me in the not-too-distant future. I look forward to that day, as I sense it will mark the completion of my transformation from human, to mother, to human-mother.

Cheers,
Ashe

Delivery Status Notification (failure)
There was a problem delivering your message to
do-not-reply@highstreetsalon.com.au
Email address could not be found

PEGGY

'Mackenport,' said Noreen, the maternal and child health nurse, a woman in her late sixties with a thick Irish accent.

'That's the one,' I said. 'Diana Mackenport.'

'But you're Davenport.' Noreen looked at her clipboard and back at me. 'What on earth happened here then?'

'Oh, my partner and I blended our last names.'

'What's your partner's name?'

'Mackisack,' I said, pronouncing it *Mc-iz-ick*, in such a way that it didn't rhyme with 'hacky sack'.

'Perfectly good name, Mackisack,' said Noreen, addressing Dee Dee. 'It means "son of Isaac".

Proud Scottish name, that. What was your mother tinkin'?'

'Bah,' offered Dee Dee.

'I guess I didn't want to lose Davenport completely,' I said.

Noreen laughed pointedly. 'Your mother's a wild woman.' She tickled Dee Dee's belly.

Dee Dee squirmed out of my arms and clomped across the room to the toy box.

'Hardwood floors at home then?' enquired Noreen, addressing me now, but studying her notebook.

'Oh . . . yes, actually.'

'Mmm-hmm.' She clicked her pen and scribbled something illegible in the margin. 'And how much milk's she drinkin'? Two to three bottles a day, I presume?'

'Actually, we've stopped giving her bottles.'

'Right answer. No bottles after the first birthday. Your mother's a clever girl, Diana.'

It dawned on me that Noreen was The Riddler in drawstring pants and a floral blouse. I bristled lightly.

When I told my father Sam and I were blending our last names he grieved on behalf of Sam's father, whom, Dad presumed, would mourn the death of their centuries-old family name, though in reality he didn't seem to mind. Sam's mother was more diplomatic, sharing that she never felt the need to give her children her last name, which she kept after marriage, because she could *feel* they were hers. Mackenport was a punchline to some. When I shared it with a colleague he wept tears of laughter. But by far the most common response was surprise that we were 'allowed' to do it, to which I'd reply that people were allowed to name their children any way they saw fit. In fact, we were considering Topel Thepatriarchy for our next child if we had one, and they were welcome to use it.

Privately, it was my father's sentiment that resonated most. I worried that my children would grow to feel disconnected from their ancestors, and that by rejecting both mine and Sam's last names I had severed their roots and sent them drifting into the ether, lost in history. Interestingly, in all the conversations we had, the loss of Davenport never came up, almost as if I had no claim to it to begin with. Davenport was my 'maiden' name, according to the bank's security questionnaire. It was my mother's by marriage and my father's by birth. He gave it to his sons and loaned it to his daughters and wives.

What on earth happened here then?

I should have asked Noreen why my own last name didn't feel like mine at all. Before kids I'd never questioned whether it was. I'd kept it after marriage without a second thought, but never once considered giving it to my children. I'd believed our surname combination to be a progressive choice, but in fact I'd taken my place in a long line of female ancestors whose names weren't theirs to give. The paternal naming tradition vanquished maternal names with each new generation, as casually as one might snip a loose thread from a garment.

'My great grandmother Peggy had more married names during her lifetime than anybody knows for sure,' I might have said to Noreen, attempting to illuminate a point flickering dimly in my mind. 'She used to joke that she changed her husband with her hairstyle. The line killed until alcoholism slurred her speech.'

I imagined Noreen being thrown at first by the departure from her regular program of riddlin' and trickery, but her interest piqued at the prospect of a challenge.

'A wayward woman, by the sounds of things,' she might have offered, feigning kindness. 'How her children must have worried.'

'She only had one,' I'd say, 'my grandmother Shirley, who was born without a name altogether. Peggy adopted her when she was six weeks old from the Salvation Army.'

'They're called Magdalene Laundries where I come from,' Noreen would jeer. 'Safe to say your grandmother was the daughter of another lost soul. Yes, I'm starting to get the picture now. Suddenly Mackisack doesn't sound so bad, eh Diana?'

Dee Dee would respond by swiftly removing her nappy and relieving herself on the carpet of Noreen's office. It would be a solid, singular turd, a detail that would offer Noreen only the most fleeting sense of relief. In a startling demonstration of hand-eye coordination, Dee Dee would bat the thing across the room so that it rolled under a large, deep cabinet built into the back wall. I'd claim some injury or other as the reason I couldn't attempt to retrieve it, and Noreen would entertain us for the next while on her hands and knees, cursing as she tried to reach it with various objects such as her shoe, clicky pen and, eventually, a rake she would retrieve from the shed out back. It would be an unprecedented sign that at just twelve months, Dee Dee was ready to start toilet training. She would be very advanced.

Once I asked my grandmother what she loved most about Peggy and she answered, 'Every little piece of her.'

My grandfather added that years earlier, when Peggy came to stay, she went into the outhouse and he put the hose over the door.

'I turned on the tap and I said, "Fuck off".'

I almost choked on a piece of baked potato, having never figured my grandfather to be the drowning an old lady in an outhouse type.

'She was trouble, actually,' he said.

'Oh well,' said my grandmother.

'You loved her, but she used to upset you so much.'

'I did love her.'

'She was a bloody menace,' my grandfather said quietly.

At sixteen, Peggy had become pregnant to the son of a Supreme Court judge, who threatened to kill himself if she kept the baby due to the shame it would bring his family. Peggy survived a backyard abortion, but it left her infertile. She discovered afterwards that she had been carrying twins. She went on to marry a man named Gordon and together they arranged to adopt. During their visit to the orphanage, Peggy was drawn to my grandmother's cot. The baby weed down the front of Peggy's coat, which she took as a lucky sign. Peggy's tendency to follow her nose was one of a million reasons Gordon loved her. She was wild and impulsive. He was dependable, and toast.

There's a photo of Peggy and my grandmother in matching fur coats walking along a city street. My grandmother is a little girl, and a perfect doll of her mother. They're side by side with their eyes straight ahead, pulling the focus of passers-by like a seasoned double act.

'I wasn't like most five-year-olds today,' said my grandmother. '"Muum, where are you?" "Mum, when are you coming home?" I was my own person.

And I had a sixth sense for danger or anything like that.'

Peggy drifted out of Gordon's arms under the spells of violent, attractive men, always with my grandmother in tow. They went with Joe to Melbourne, Johnny to Sydney and Lenny to Port Pirie. It was the *Possum Magic* of dick, except my grandmother only wished for the power to become invisible. Johnny was a maître d' who looked like Cesar Romero. One night he was hurting Peggy and my then ten-year-old grandmother came up behind him and smashed a framed picture over his head. He chased her down the laneway wearing it as a collar, like a dashing, murderous clown. The gate with the sticky latch opened for her, but not Johnny. She ran to the sound of his fading roar, got to the train station and stole onto a carriage to Bathurst, where Gordon was stationed in the army. He smuggled her into the camp in his overcoat. The next day, peace was declared in Europe. Men cried and danced in the street with my grandmother on their shoulders. Peggy arrived the day after and took her back to Sydney, where Johnny was waiting.

'Do you resent Peggy?' I asked my grandmother over dessert.

'I used to want to change her, because I wasn't mature enough to accept her as she was. I wanted a fat plain mother like everybody else. Instead I was stuck with a villainous sexpot, slim and dark-haired with flashing eyes.'

'She was worse for wear by the time I met her,' said my grandfather.

I winced.

'Mum got old before her time. She'd been knocked around. And she was sick then, from the booze. I used to sniff it out and tip it down the sink. If I had my time again, I'd give her a bottle of brandy every day, because what are you going to do?'

My grandmother washed the dishes and I dried, keeping a safe distance from her signature dishwater, so hot you could poach an egg in it. We kept talking for a while. Later she made us cups of warm Ovaltine, like her mother would bring her every night before bed, she said. Every little piece of her. I stayed the night in the room I'd slept in as a child, dreaming of a thread from me to Peggy, drifting somewhere in the ether.

BABY'S FIRST COURT APPEARANCE

When I imagined myself as The Mother, as I was referred to on the chart hanging from the end of my hospital bed, I was cradling my newborn while singing soft lullabies, my love tumbling down on them like a shimmering colostrum waterfall. I was hypnotised, a pink-cheeked Gollum with a baby-shaped ring, my long fingers clasping the edge of her bassinet, never letting go.

In reality, when my title became official my only wish was to be wrapped in a space blanket and carried into a room reserved for witnesses of heinous crimes, stocked with tissues and Scotch Finger biscuits. There were no lullabies or shimmering waterfalls. I held and fed my baby because she cried when I didn't. Sometimes I'd rock in a ball and cover my ears instead. The days alone with her were long and uncomfortable, like there was a stranger in my space, a housemate I didn't gel with. Ordinarily, I would have remained quietly in my room when I heard them come home rather than risk an encounter. I'd have eaten a muesli bar for dinner instead of revealing myself, had their life not depended on it. I would have urinated in the water glass by my bed instead of going to the toilet.

'If people knew how bad this was,' I said to a friend two weeks after the birth, nipples flashing red like emergency lights under my dressing-gown, 'they would be sterilised on their thirteenth birthdays.'

My disdain for the job at hand grew with each passing day. I had been horrified by pregnancy and its routine takeover of my body, mind and identity at large, and the birth had been a shit show, but neither event disturbed me quite so deeply as motherhood. The hours were criminal and the wages were a joke. A sweatshop seamstress would turn up her nose. It was the sustained takeover, the eternal shit show. I wanted to take motherhood to VCAT. I wanted to open a can of Erin Brockovich on motherhood's arse.

I wrestled Dee Dee into a strict sleep schedule and baby-proofed our apartment until it resembled a padded cell. If she cried in a cafe I asked staring patrons loudly if they could hold my shopping bag or the door, a milk-stained muslin wrapped around each of my fists. I clapped back at every piece of unsolicited parenting advice, which was constant, and never failed to enrage and humiliate, the way it caked on me like regurgitated milk.

Six weeks after the birth, I was pulled over for driving with my phone in my lap.

Officer Marks was unmoved by the fact that I was a new mother who was braving the morning traffic.

'Licence, please,' he said flatly.

'You're not going to fine me, are you?' I asked, tears already rolling from my sleepless eyes. 'Please, I just had a baby. I'm so sorry. I'm just really overwhelmed.'

'Licence, please,' he said.

I handed it to him through the window. 'Does that mean . . . you're going to fine me?'

'That is correct.'

When Officer Marks spoke, not a muscle was activated except the ones that made his mouth form the words. Even those were barely perceptible, a slight contraction of his top lip midway through the word 'correct'. The faintest twitch.

'But isn't it like five hundred dollars?' I asked, tear ducts suddenly bone dry.

'That. Is. Correct,' he repeated.

'Just so I'm clear, you could waive this fine but you're choosing to give it to me. Is that what's happening here?'

He delivered his catchphrase once more.

In my fantasy version of the events that followed, I delivered a vehement and devastating speech on the many ways Officer Marks's lack of empathy contributed to the problems facing mothers today. I illuminated with grace and precision that the 'special treatment' I was seeking was nothing more than the slightest recognition of my contribution to society: a brand-spanking-new member in return for eighteen weeks minimum wage and my body, mind and life as I knew it. A light flickered behind his beady eyes. I'm so sorry, he whispered, before balling up the fine and pushing it into his loveless, chapped mouth, both of us nodding as he chewed and eventually swallowed the wad of injustice in one painful-looking gulp.

In reality, Officer Marks gave me the fine and I screamed obscenities at him from the window as I drove away.

Dee Dee had started to cry.

'Please don't do this to me,' I muttered. 'Please, I'm begging you. Not now.'

I made it to the cafe, where my friend endured a play by play of my suffering at the hands of the sadistic police officer. Dee Dee slept peacefully in her capsule under the table, lulled by the din of the restaurant.

'The way he pressed his face up against the window and peered in at the phone, which was between my legs by the way. It was predatory!'

'Mmmm, you mentioned that,' my friend replied, reaching for her wallet.

'And that catchphrase! Can you imagine? Gassing up a new mother like that.'

'Such a dick,' she said, placing a twenty-dollar bill on the table.

'I'm not paying that fine. I'll go to court if I have to.'

'Why not!' she replied. 'Hey, I've got to run. How's mum life, anyway?'

'Total bliss,' I said, massaging my jaw.

After she left I ordered another coffee and got to work on my letter of appeal.

To whom it may concern,

There is a disgraceful lack of support for mothers in Australia: in the workforce, maternity wards, childcare system and, most recently, in my unfortunate experience, on the Victorian roads.

My baby is five weeks old, so as you might imagine I barely know what day it is, let alone the fact that I had absent-mindedly rested my phone on my lap before starting the car.

Far from showing any understanding for my situation, Officer Marks seemed to take great pleasure in administering the $480 fine that I am contesting today. It's almost a week's worth of maternity leave. What if I didn't have a supportive, financially stable partner and that was my only source of income? How would I hypothetically have made rent this week?

Statistics show my earning potential will plateau when I do eventually return to work, while my husband's will continue to rise. As a primary carer, I will contribute countless hours of unpaid work that will both further his career and help keep the nation's economy running smoothly.

I hope you can show me the regard that Officer Marks could not and waive this fine given my vulnerable and entirely selfless position as a full-time, soon-to-be unpaid carer.

Thanking you in advance,
Ashe Davenport

When the letter of rejection came, I decided my case would be better argued in person, where a judge could experience the full effect of my vulnerable selflessness.

I appealed without delay and received notice of my court date.

On the day of the hearing, I washed the sour milk out of my hair and dressed Dee Dee in her most respectable pyjamas. My bag was packed for battle: mobile phone records, birth documents, proof of income, women's unpaid labour stats, study on the effects of sleep deprivation, nappies, wipes, dummy.

While waiting to be called in the packed courtroom, I listened to a case involving a man who owed $17,000 in tram fines and was accompanied by a full-time mental health carer. After him was a single mother of three who had her payment suspended because she'd been unable to attend a government-enforced playgroup.

When my name was called, I pushed the pram through the narrow aisle to the table at the front of the room.

'Good morning, Ms Davenport,' said the judge. 'I'm only vaguely interested in what you have to say for yourself.'

Things were off to a shaky start.

'As a mother,' I began, gesturing to Dee Dee, 'I will likely experience a seventeen per cent loss of wages across my lifetime. And for what crime should I endure this penalty? Why, the most passionate one of them all: the crime of loving someone other than myself.'

The judge took off her glasses and rubbed her eyes. 'What exactly does this have to do with you being fined for breaking the law, Ms Davenport?'

I cleared my throat. 'As you can see from these phone records . . .' I emptied the nappy bag on the table and the wipes slid off the edge and onto the carpet. 'They're here somewhere . . . Um, my phone wasn't in use anywhere near the time of the incident. It was simply on my seat—between my legs, actually—'

'Driving with a phone on your seat is illegal,' said the judge.

'I think the lack of consideration demonstrated by Officer Marks is part of a much larger problem in our society: the routine disregard of mothers' contribution to it.'

'I'm surprised you were expecting consideration given some of the language you used with Officer Marks. I would play a sample of the recording, but there are students present.'

I opened my mouth and closed it again. Dee Dee kicked her legs and squealed with what sounded like delight.

'I believe you have a victim mentality, Ms Davenport,' said the judge. 'Pay the fine and please remove yourself from my courtroom.'

The squeak of the pram wheels was deafening as I made my way to the exit, through the rows of people awaiting their hearings. The security guard offered to hold the door, but I declined out of sheer embarrassment.

Did I just get Judge Judy'd? I wondered in the baby change room by the lift, holding Dee Dee close. I thought of the mother of three laying out her case, and the way she apologised when her phone rang, so matter-of-factly, no time for self-righteousness, though she had every right. I peered into the stainless-steel panel nailed above the basin in place of a mirror. Reflected back at me was the blurred, featureless outline of a woman with child. A lump of clay awaiting construction.

FLAT SPOT

When puberty came and went without leaving me a single breast, I became fixated on what I considered my most glaring physical flaw. My friend Sarah at least got one. She had to wear a prosthetic bra with a flesh-coloured gel filling on one side, but nonetheless I was painfully jealous of her. She did, after all, require a bra.

'You really don't have much, do you!' said Carole, the sales assistant of Bonne Nuit, the lingerie shop near our family home in Bayside.

She and my mother chortled from either side of the change room curtain.

'Just little budding breasts at this stage,' answered

my mother. 'They hurt when you play netball, don't they darl?'

'Mu-u-um,' I managed over the lump in my throat, eyes locked on my fourteen-year-old reflection, the puffy swollen nipples on the otherwise flat chest. An absurd nipple-to-breast ratio, I remember thinking. Like a small boy with an oestrogen imbalance. I winced as Carole's measuring tape brushed past them then recoiled into her pocket.

'I might have a sports bra that'll fit,' she said, leaving the curtain open as she bustled through the small, jumbled store.

My heart sank. I'd been hoping for a bra with padding, but knowing my mother probably wouldn't approve, was prepared to settle for something with a bow or some lace—anything that would help me feel even remotely feminine in that area.

Carole returned with a sturdy black crop top with thick straps, fit for an eight-year-old gymnast.

'It's not worth trying on,' she said, ushering my mother towards the counter. 'Unless you want to, love?'

I shook my head dumbly from the cubicle, releasing a hand from one of my buds to close the curtain.

'And it's on sale,' said Carole.

'Lucky me,' my mother replied. 'Listen, Carole, her sister's almost out of the last bra you fit her in.'

'Oh, wow,' she said. 'Well, bring her back in. That's what I'm here for.'

Dressed, I mumbled something about the milk bar next door, and once outside I started to run, past the fish-and-chip shop, beauty salon where I'd get my first Brazilian wax, and hairdressers that would keep me in blonde foils for the remainder of my teens. Past my old primary school, along the street where boys would follow me home, throwing lemons at me and chanting, 'Surfboard! Surfboard!', a taunt inspired by my flat chest and our suburb's proximity to the beach.

(A small detour . . . Rumour had it that one of my tormentors had taped my name to his bedroom wall and when his mother ordered him to take it down it took the paint with it, leaving a memory of me permanently enshrined above his bed. He liked me—isn't that sweet? He even asked me to the year six dance. I laughed, then he spat on my shoe. Years later, he went to jail. It was for an unrelated offence, but even still, I like to think I was at least partly responsible for the direction his life would take.)

I pushed past my ample-bosomed sister in the hallway, slammed my bedroom door and released the sob that had been building for a kilometre. Posters of Zac Hanson and Claudia Schiffer watched over me from their blu-tacked stations on my wall, a subliminal reminder that if I had the body of a 23-year-old supermodel, one of the pocket-sized middle-parted boys in my class might choose me as their girlfriend.

There was a knock at the door. My mother's voice.

'Can I come in?'

'GO. AWAY. MUM.'

She took that as a yes.

I remained facing the wall as my bed creaked with her weight on the end of it.

'I never had much in the way of breasts,' she said.

'Yeah, and now you have fake ones,' I said.

'I breastfed four children! My nipples looked like fingers.'

'Yuck! I'm definitely not breastfeeding. And I'm getting a boob job.'

'Oh, get a grip, your body's just starting to develop. And it's a beautiful body.'

'Ewwwww, Mum! Can you please get out?'

My body would develop, but not in the way I hoped. My torso remained flat on all four sides, a shoebox in which to store my broken heart. On the upside, my arse was flat too, which was a covetable trait at a time when women asked if their bums looked big in fear that the answer would be yes. I'd been blessed with two tiny pancakes to fill the back of my ultra-low-rise jeans. At least that would never go out of style.

Our household was not a religious one, but for the purpose of acquiring a rack I turned to God. Every night, in my church of child stars and supermodels, I'd kneel at my window and barter with the sky. I wasn't a greedy girl, I didn't need DDs; a nice full B cup would suffice. I'd seen *Weird Science*, I understood that anything more than a handful was a waste. And that my body existed to fulfil the fantasies of teenage boys so that I could be their slave.

On the cusp of my 21st birthday I arranged a private meeting with my father at his light-filled home in a leafy, inner-city suburb. In my backpack was just over $500 in savings from my catering job, which I planned to tip onto my father's coffee table at the crescendo of my presentation. Next to it was a plastic binder of research on the safety of breast augmentation and the rising popularity of the procedure.

'I'll pay, love,' he said on page two of the binder. 'I had no idea you were so ... distressed by this.'

I blew my nose. My tears had arrived earlier than planned.

'I'm too embarrassed to go swimming! Or take my clothes off in front of my boyfriend. I'm deformed!'

Had I confided this in a plastic surgeon's office they might have suspected I was suffering from body dysmorphic disorder (BDD) and referred me to a therapist. In a sense they would have been right to do so.

I was a AAA cup with D cup nips, they were the facts, but I was clocking up several hours of obsession a day, wishing on stars, praying to a God I knew nothing about, and staring at myself from different angles in every reflective surface I came across. I had a collection of bras with plastic airbags sewn into the lining and enough chicken fillets to fill a Barbie Dream-House. I refused to sleep on my stomach, my favourite sleeping position, out of fear that it would stunt my breast growth. I was a likely candidate for BDD. I was also a *Cosmopolitan* subscriber and very vain.

Like a surgeon, my father processed the information presented to him with confidence, only through several filters of subjectivity—stacked, I assume, in the following order: Love, Guilt, Maleness, Disposable Income. A numerical solution to a messy emotional problem appealed to him, and here was an opportunity to fix his daughter's pain for x amount of dollars, minus the twenty-dollar notes spilling off his table.

'Come here, duck,' he said, pulling me into his mist of aftershave and cigarette smoke.

He made an appointment with his wife's plastic surgeon and I returned to my share house to flit from room to room, incapable of sitting still.

Almost ten years would pass before I considered how implants would affect my ability to breastfeed, around the time when I was breastfeeding my newborn. I had a vague memory of the surgeon saying it would be fine, but I couldn't have cared less at the time. As it turned out, the system worked—thankfully, due to the convenience of breastfeeding, and regretfully, due to the excruciating pain of it in the beginning.

'I think she needs feeding,' Sam would say in the early weeks following Dee Dee's arrival, after an unsuccessful attempt to calm her.

Usually, he'd utter this bone-chilling sentence from the doorway of the bedroom, in which I'd be recovering from the last round of cluster-feeding in filthy sheets, the room dark and littered with bloodied chemist stock.

'I dare you to say that to me again,' I'd whisper, spinning my head around 360 degrees to face him.

At our eight-week check-up, the nurse pointed out a flat spot on the back of Dee Dee's head. I hadn't noticed it before, but it came sharply into focus.

'Does she favour a particular side when she sleeps?' she asked.

'Umm ...' I pictured Dee Dee in her sleep suit in the bassinet, her neck crooked slightly to the left. 'I think so.'

'It can happen during pregnancy or birth, but don't worry, it's only cosmetic. It won't affect her brain development. Is she doing tummy time? The more tummy time you can do, the better ...'

I nodded as she spoke, while behind her posters of round-headed babies giggled at my inadequacy. I had the distinct feeling that I was sinking to the bottom of a pool. This was clearly my fault. Dee Dee hated tummy time, so I rarely encouraged it. And my stress during the pregnancy and birth couldn't have helped, all that tension pressing on her skull like last year's swimming cap. Blame sunk into my body and anchored itself under my ribcage. *Only cosmetic.* Two months in and I'd mangled my daughter's head, like a doll left carelessly in the driveway.

'It's a moderate case,' the nurse was saying, 'which means she might be eligible for a corrective helmet.'

I couldn't understand how I'd been entrusted with something so precious. Who allowed it to happen? Why was everybody pretending I was even remotely qualified for the job? I was living in an altered reality, a stark intimate play with all the exits bolted shut. The audience shifting uncomfortably as I stumbled through my lines opposite my demanding but charismatic co-star who got all the applause.

An appointment was made with a local physiotherapist who would assess the severity of Dee Dee's flat spot. The midwife completed her scene, waving me off in a gesture of good faith that I'd make it the three blocks home without warping my baby into the shape of a triangle.

That evening, I immersed myself in the experiences of strangers online. HeyHeyitsSarah was adamant that Flat Head Syndrome could be prevented by holding babies more and never letting them sleep in the car seat. She had five children with 'beautifully round heads'. The trick was never to make an appointment further than you could carry them. And to ensure you loved them enough to do so. MummyMarcia suggested we go back to sleeping our babies on their stomachs to give the backs of their heads a better chance to develop. DirtyFreda replied that SIDs cases had dropped drastically since the advice changed to back sleeping, and an increase in flatter-shaped heads was a small price to pay. Lizzy09 chimed in to accuse MummyMarcia of attempted genocide.

Dee Dee wasn't eligible for a helmet—at least one that wasn't going to cost thousands of dollars—but with a little time, osteopathy and hair growth, the spot became invisible to the untrained eye. Meanwhile, I continued to monitor it with a private intensity, taking countless photos of her head from different angles and zooming in on her facial features for evidence of asymmetry, which could be a side effect of the condition. I repositioned her while she slept, sometimes several times a night, and agonised over whether to fork out the money for a corrective helmet I'd been advised she didn't really need.

Months later, I found myself back in my childhood suburb standing outside Bonne Nuit. The shop was as overstocked and disorganised as I remembered, the air just as laden with potpourri. Inside I was greeted by a silver-haired woman in a billowy dress with a measuring tape draped around her shoulders.

'Carole's no longer with us,' she said. 'Long gone now.'

'Dead?' I gulped a licorice bullet from the milk bar next door.

'Oh no, dear! We play golf every Thursday. She's no longer with the company.'

I nodded, dismayed that I wouldn't get to have my full circle healing moment with Carole, and slightly annoyed that she had a narrative outside of being a prominent figure in my journey to body acceptance. After I'd driven all that way.

'She might remember me,' I said. 'I was the girl who ran crying out of the shop in the late nineties.'

The woman—Helen, according to her name tag—chuckled. 'I can't say that would narrow it down all that much.'

'Right-o.' I folded my arms across my chest.

I was glad to hear Carole's reign of terror had finally come to an end. Her cutting remarks delivered with the lightness of air had no place around emotionally fragile teenagers. I imagined she would fare well psyching out her competitors on the golf course.

'Fittings generally take place at pivotal moments in a person's life,' said Helen. 'First fittings, after surgery, cancer, breastfeeding, weight loss or gain. You name it. We see it all in here.'

She tugged an end of the measuring tape so that it slithered along the back of her neck.

'Now,' she said, regarding my chest like a builder sizing up a wall for a spice rack, 'what can I do for you today?'

It was time for a new bra. My pre-maternity bralettes no longer applied to the situation, having been designed for tits that stayed up on their own. Breastfeeding had swollen, stretched and deflated them into something new. They had needs now, a new house built just for them, where they could rest and be held.

'Oh, nothing for me, thank you,' I said, and wished Helen goodbye.

I took my business to L'amour a few suburbs over. Bonne Nuit would have to pry my wallet from my cold, dead hands.

PARENTS' GROUP

It was a Wednesday and our third trip to the zoo that week. Dee Dee was asleep in the baby carrier, which left me free to engage in meaningful catch-ups with all the friends I'd made during my first year of motherhood. Naturally I felt closest to the orangutans, but the wombats offered a sturdy shoulder to cry on. The Sumatran tiger was nothing short of an inspiration, the way she stalked the outline of her enclosure on her unrelenting quest for freedom, occasionally allowing herself a moment of quiet contemplation on her bed of straw.

'I'm so lonely,' I whispered to her once through the glass.

She turned away from me and groaned, suggesting, perhaps, that I didn't know from lonely.

I'd lost touch with my parents' group some months earlier.

'Everything's going well, touch wood,' a woman said during our first meeting, gently knocking on her head, as if underneath her hair was a wooden wig stand.

I smiled, wincing. My daughter was eight weeks old. Everything was going like I'd been hit in the face with a brick.

'Hubby says ...' began another woman, and I promptly flicked the safety switch in my brain.

I attended the meetings infrequently and often left the group on read on our WhatsApp thread entitled 'Lattes and Lullabies'. I was naive, and thought I could be discerning when it came to parent friends who lived within walking distance of my house. I didn't know the first year of stay-at-home motherhood was a game of emotional *Survivor*, and without alliances you were cast onto your own little island of darkness.

My sense of isolation really came into its own after we moved. Dee Dee was three months old and as riveting a conversationalist as a ham wearing clothes. While Sam was at work, I manoeuvred her around our new suburb, hoping to stumble across my tribe of parent friends.

'How does existential dread factor into your life now that you're a mum?' I wanted to ask casually by the swings. Or, 'How much do you resent your partner on a scale of one to six million?'

But more often than not, I said nothing, painfully aware that most of the parents had established their tribes already. In the rare event that I engaged in conversation, things never evolved past, 'Hello' and 'How old is your little one?'

Don't come on too strong, I'd remind myself. Don't cry and do not under any circumstances scream, 'HELP! PLEASE! ANYBODY!'

'We're going to head off,' I'd say. 'Busy, busy, busy, aren't we, Dee Dee? Bye!'

In most cases, I was definitely about to cry.

Lone parents seemed to gravitate towards the zoo, especially on weekday mornings. We were less self-conscious there. Family vehicles would dot the length of the mostly empty car park like planets in the solar system. We trickled in when the gates opened, keeping a respectful distance from one another, while inside the enclosures the animals would stir peacefully, suspended in the moment between waking and remembering where they were.

'Back again!' said the woman at the ticket booth as she scanned my annual family pass.

'Ha ha, yup,' I said, hesitating, wanting to joke that

I'd slept in my car, but unsure if it would sound weird-funny or weird-concerning.

Dee Dee stirred in the carrier and I began shifting my weight from side to side.

'I remember that move,' said the woman. 'It became so second nature, I'd do it with loaves of bread!'

We laughed.

'I do that too!' I said. 'Wow. We have actual brain damage.'

'All worth it, though,' she said, and was still while she waited for my answer.

Oh, totally, I agreed and wished her a great day.

All worth it, I mused to the ring-tailed lemurs, *is the sentimental equivalent of a ball gag*. It was the conclusion to every 'motherhood is hard'-type article I'd read online. If I objected, I'd be forced to admit that I didn't love my child enough to justify the sacrifice. Not only to my brain capacity, but to my sleep, breasts, career, individual goals, sex life, social life, abdominal muscles and the ability to sneeze without peeing my pants a little bit. Incredibly, in the space of just three months, I'd found that Dee Dee was in fact all worth it, but what did that make me? To become a mother, this laundry list of sacrifice was just a basic, entry-level requirement. No questions asked. It made me doubt how valuable the items were to begin with.

The mother lemur was balancing a baby on her

back while picking bits of popcorn out of a pine cone, an enrichment provided by the zoo to assist her in staving off insanity. I could relate. During Dee Dee's nap times at home I had taken to polishing the sauce bottles and stalking childless friends on the internet. It was important to stay sharp.

The baby slid off its mother and clambered onto a neighbouring lemur, which shrugged it off and began grooming it.

'Lemurs take turns caring for a new infant in the group,' intoned a pre-recorded voiceover. 'This behaviour is called "alloparenting". It allows mothers to rest and babies to gain valuable social skills. Please dispose of your rubbish in the bins provided.'

A small crowd of onlookers had already gathered at the giraffe enclosure. Elegant and popular, people travelled from all over to bask in their glow.

'What a masterpiece of creation,' remarked a woman breathlessly. 'You're amazing, you're exquisite.'

I rolled my eyes. I resented the giraffes, yet I couldn't stay away. Like the white-linen-clad mothers I followed on Instagram who homeschooled their nine children in huts in Byron Bay, the giraffes appeared naturally composed under pressure. The trio of zebras that shared their enclosure were often at their ankles, kicking pettily at each other, but the giraffes never batted an eyelid.

'I love you!' shouted someone from the crowd.

'Don't encourage them,' I muttered as I walked away.

The wombats were fast asleep in their glass-cased burrow, buried underground yet exposed to the world. I was disappointed not to see them in action, but appreciated their powerful statement on the effects of social media on the postnatally depressed.

On the orangutan observation deck, I fed Dee Dee, while on the other side of the glass Mawar, the adult female of the group, was organising brightly coloured strips of fabric. It was her enrichment du jour. Her long fingers glided across each piece, folding it in half, smoothing it with her palm, then placing it carefully in a pile. Occasionally she would arrange a piece of cloth over her shoulder, as if she were trying on a scarf. Then quickly she would remove it, suddenly aware that she had nowhere to go.

The lemurs were having a popcorn party and Mawar got lumped with the folding. I made a mental note to send an email to the complaints department on her behalf entitled: *Laundry is not an enrichment.* As far as I was concerned, it was the antichrist. My house had resembled a ransacked laundromat since Dee Dee was born. Miscellaneous cloth squares hung stiffly over the backs of chairs, beach towels soaked in buckets and sheets draped the doors. Eventually everything would make its way to the pile on the kitchen table, a boulder of fabric so large and enduring that it made me question the meaning of life. On rare occasions, when the moon was full and the night bird sounded her majestic call, there would be a lull in the washing cycle and the table would be clear. The gleaming surface whispered the promise of a dinner party with human friends, Sam pouring the wine and me contributing valuable insights about the kind of important global issues not covered on huggies.com. It triggered memories of lazy Sundays before we were parents; newspapers and pastry crumbs strewn across its surface, mementos of a decadent world of free time and print media . . . then the dryer would beep and the fantasy dissolved. And once again I would find myself faced with the mountain of folding, aware of my conjunctivitis and the chemist closing at five.

Dee Dee was asleep in the carrier again. Her bare feet flopped gently with each of my steps. We passed a group of mothers sitting on the grass. They were sipping from enormous takeaway cups while their children rolled shrieking down a nearby hill.

'What day is it?' I overheard one of the women ask.

'Wednesday,' answered another.

'I'm so tired,' she said. 'Harris woke me up at four this morning by sticking his entire finger up my nose.'

I gasped. *Did you lock him in the cellar?* I wanted to ask. *Or give him raw liver for breakfast instead of Weet-Bix? What's the appropriate punishment for digital assault in the dead of night?*

'Mmmm,' murmured another woman in the group, 'Greta loves that move.'

'I'm just . . . exhausted,' said her friend.

'Mmmm,' the women murmured in unison.

I looked over to where known offenders Greta and Harris played freely in the sunshine. Meanwhile their mothers were engaged in a group trauma counselling session on the grass. I longed for a social environment where there was no limit to the number of times I could say how tired I was. If the price was a nasal fingering at 4 a.m., I would pay that price.

At the spider monkey enclosure, a package had been given to the tenants for their enrichment, a box filled with straw and cucumber skins. The monkeys screeched and swung from the ropes, energised by their renewed sense of purpose. I was reminded that my delivery of hypoallergenic laundry detergent was scheduled for that afternoon and figured it was time to get going.

Joan the cassowary was our last visit for the day. She'd recently moved to her own enclosure, and was grooming herself in the window when we arrived. A descendant of dinosaurs, her wedged casque and dagger-like claws had equipped her for an ancient and brutal world. Her huge yellow eyes glowed from the electric blue skin of her face and a long red gland hung from her neck like jewels.

Oh, it's you, she said, with a brief glance.

I asked if she was enjoying her time alone. With Joan I found it best to get straight to the point.

She plucked a bug from deep within her feathers, tossed it to the back of her throat and said, *Alone is the only way to be, if you're that way inclined.*

I asked her what she did with so much time to herself.

I admire the dregs of the world's beauty, she replied, inspecting her middle claw.

I nodded and held Dee Dee's feet lightly. What do you find most beautiful about it? I asked.

The outline of a new moon in a clear blue sky, she snapped.

A baby cried in the distance and Joan extended her long neck. I looked over my shoulder and saw a woman approaching with a pram. When I turned back, Joan was gone.

'Shhhh shhhh shhhh,' said the woman, rolling her pram back and forth over a grate, a collage of coffee stains on her t-shirt. 'Please, please sleep.'

'Hi,' I said. 'Are you okay?'

'No,' she said.

We laughed.

'Are you?' she asked.

'Oh, definitely not,' I said.

We laughed again, shyly at first then deliriously, with the occasional snort from both parties. Her baby stopped crying and we introduced ourselves, while somewhere in the foliage Joan hissed approvingly.

BUSH BABY

Rosemary wished there was something she could do, given we were travelling with a baby and about to miss our flight. There was an issue with the website we booked the tickets through, she said. It was completely out of her hands and no, we would not be eligible for a refund. I said Dee Dee was getting restless in the pram and needed to be taken for a stroll; there was a good chance that I was about to start aggressively calling her 'darling'. This was Sam's department. People go out of their way to help him. He has an apologetic charm and the eyes of a baby deer. He also has endless patience when it comes to bureaucracy, which stems from a bloody-minded desire to conquer it. Rosemary was toast.

Sam is a product of his parents, kind, immaculately mannered New Zealanders and firm believers in the value of a stiff upper lip. I am also a product of my parents, emotionally volatile Australians whose manners can be traced to an Irish pub brawl. Sam and I acknowledge the value in each other's emotional code and the problems within our own, yet secretly believe that if it were a choice between one or the other, ours is by far superior.

Vulnerability is strength, I might argue.

Emotional resilience is fundamental, he might retort.

Sure enough, when I returned to the check-in desk Rosemary was aglow with the feeling of helping an endearing deer-eyed man get his family on the next available flight at minimal cost.

You win this round, emotional decorum, I smiled, *if only for your cost-effectiveness.*

It seemed unnatural, a baby with a passport, adorable but absurd, like a guinea pig with a bank account. We were heading to New Zealand to stay with Sam's family at their house in Lake Rotoiti. I'd been there once before, back when I was footloose and episiotomy scar-free. I had been fascinated by the way Sam's family did things together, cheerfully and without complaint. Every meal, every team-centred physical activity. Each morning we would set off single file to accomplish something together: a bushwalk along a predetermined route, fishing or a day of water sports. As a general rule, I try to avoid being dragged behind a speeding vehicle by a string, and so on the water sports day, I passed up my turn to wakeboard.

'Maybe next time!' I said, trying my best to ignore the wave of disappointment that rippled through the boat. I squeezed myself into the bow and took a seat next to Sam's mother.

'It's really not my thing either,' said Bridget. 'I just enjoy watching the boys have their fun.'

She retrieved a salad roll from the esky beneath her seat and peeled back the cling wrap.

'That said, I used to water-ski when they were younger, just to show them I could do it.'

My stomach growled, but Bridget didn't seem to hear it. She took a bite of her bap and regarded me placidly. *You must earn our respect*, I imagined her saying, *Then, and only then, may you join me in the dining quarters of this water vessel.*

'You know what?' I ventured. 'I will give it a go! YOLO, right?'

The approval was palpable as I was laced into the hammered-down boots and lowered into the cold black water. For a moment, I basked in the vision of myself as a team player that shone in the eyes of the people aboard. I was a keep calm, carry on wakeboarding sort of woman, a fine specimen indeed, that is, until the engine roared.

After three failed attempts, each more terrifying than the last, I figured I'd at least earned myself a roll.

'I think I'm done now,' I said, bobbing helplessly in the water in my shackle and life vest.

'C'mon, you almost got up that time!' Sam's brother yelled brightly.

'You can do it!' they urged. 'Don't worry about us. We'll just keep going until you nail it!'

'But my shoulder hurts,' I said in a small voice, 'and I don't want to.'

They hauled me back on board and took turns offering words of solace.

'There's always tomorrow,' said Bridget, giving my arm a squeeze. 'Now, who's ready for lunch?'

My family holidays were less of a team sport and more of an individual showcase. We enjoyed the odd meal together or spot of gossip by the pool, but outside of doing and saying whatever best catered to our particular needs at any given moment, there was little in the way of an itinerary. My family are a super-group of moderately talented prima donnas who have no issue showing up to rehearsal sulky, snarky or fresh from cutting up a fellow band member's sequined gown.

★

'Our families are like the characters in *Downton Abbey*,' I mused over a glass of airport wine. 'Yours are the people being polite in the drawing room and mine are sweating in the kitchen with their hearts on their sleeves.'

'Your family wouldn't last a week as servants,' said Sam. 'You guys would be out in the woods fighting each other with knives.'

'Now that's a show I'd watch.'

In the beginning, I found Sam's family's brand of upbeat togetherness refreshing. I learned that keeping my feelings private could be a power. I could shield myself from hurtful opinions. I could preserve my energy and give more thoughtful responses. I became a better listener. Smiling through dinners at Sam's parents' house when I'd had a bad day felt regal and hardcore. Sure, it was a little stifling at times, but the feeling was mild enough to ignore. It wasn't until I became a parent that the expectation I adhere to their emotional code began to feel like wearing a raincoat inside a hot car.

The Rotoiti house backed onto the clear blue lake, separated from the cloudless sky by a zigzag of surrounding mountains. Boats bobbed next to private jetties. Hydrangeas burst along the driveway, their scent helping to mask the notes of rotten egg due to the sulphur rising from the earth. The surrounding area boasted three active volcanoes. The constant potential for natural disaster was unnerving, but, on the upside, the house featured its own geothermal hot pool, no gas or electricity required. The lake was an ancient crater, 80 metres deep and filled with water, fish and eels. The eels were a protected species. Many of them were female and over a century old. One could only imagine the secrets.

On the first night, we shared good news over freshly caught whitebait. The group planned to go out on the boat together the following morning for a day of water sports. Dee Dee would love being on the boat, they said. I smiled and said what a shame it was about her recent ear infection and the doctor's orders to avoid water where possible. (Children are a precious gift in many ways, like how they come with an eighteen-year pass to get out of doing anything you don't want to do.)

Dee Dee and I waved them off from the shore the following morning, lying slug-like on a blanket on the grass. She gazed wistfully at my keys, her favourite plaything, which I'd placed just out of her reach in an attempt to encourage her to crawl. She extended a chubby arm, kicked her legs a couple of times, then promptly quit, and became engrossed in some blades of grass a more reasonable distance away.

I looked out at the lake as Sam's younger brother lowered his girlfriend in for her initiation. Her long hair had flowed in the wind as the boat left the jetty, but now it was tied in a stiff ponytail atop her head. She nodded solemnly from her starting crouch position and the engine sounded its fury. I wondered if Dee Dee would grow up to be interested in wakeboarding—outside of it being a vehicle through which she would try to win her father's approval, obviously.

Inside, family photographs crowded the surfaces and walls. Sam had spent his childhood holidays here, donut-ing and wakeboarding and fishing. A Māori family used to live in the house next door. The kids would go out on the boat with Sam and his brothers and whichever cousins were around. A white guy named Gary had since bought the place. He lived there alone and seemed to like it that way. Sam's mother was one of seven children, all of whom had children, some of whose children now had children. Large framed photo collages hung in the stairwell, like a Magic Eye of winning smiles and long legs. They were an intelligent and fertile breed, and there were just so many of them. I feared total absorption was inevitable. My daughter was already a fully-fledged member of the clan, but I considered myself an outsider, a carriage to bring forth more leggy brains. Since being married I qualified for the 'outlaws' photo at family gatherings, where I stood alongside Sam's father and the other partners, my countrymen within a country.

Wasn't having children itself a declaration of independence? I wondered, tipping a nautical-themed puzzle onto the kitchen table. *Were Sam and I not two equal parties that had come together to form an entirely new one? Did not yellow and blue make green?* In all likelihood, we'd follow in the footsteps of our parents and their parents before them. We'd cherrypick the things we liked from the way we were raised and make our own mistakes along the way. I separated the edges of the jigsaw and mentally began to sketch our code of conduct: Self-control, yes; repression, no. Emotional expression, yes; knife fighting, no.

The group returned for a lunch of cold chicken, white wine and salads left over from the night before. We ate under a large cream umbrella erected on the back deck. The sun was pale and welcoming. The breeze was oh-so-subtle and refreshing.

I jumped at the sight of a man walking down the side of the house. He was big and tattooed, and wore a towel printed with tropical fish around his shoulders.

'Didn't mean to alarm you, folks!' he said. 'This was my family's house. Gary said I can swim here whenever I want.'

'No worries, bro,' rippled around the table.

The man sprung from the end of the jetty with an

almighty splash. He swam out a little then floated on his back, arms outstretched to the sky. The conversation around the table had resumed some moments earlier. I scanned their faces for evidence of discomfort or shame, but nothing seemed out of the ordinary. Sam's family were self-proclaimed Pākehā, a Māori word meaning White Fellas or New Zealanders of European descent. Rotoiti was stolen land. Sam's family were foreigners too.

After two days of successfully avoiding water sports, I agreed to join the group on a bushwalk. Rolls packed and Baby Bjorned, the eight of us set off single file up the mountain. Trees stretched 50 metres into the air, their crowns joined at the top, locking us into a sphere of humid green. It was majestic, but disorientating, particularly for Dee Dee. The further we went, the more distressed she became. In a low persistent wail she demanded to know where we had taken her. And where we thought we got off, changing the sky from blue to green. We tried facing her in and out of the baby carrier, giving her a bottle, holding, shushing, singing, but it was no use. The narrow path plummeted to our right. The ground level, where the car was parked, became further away with every step. I suggested turning back, but my request was declined via a collective reassurance that she would settle. So on we marched to the sound of Dee Dee's monotone grizzle that lodged itself deep in the muscles of my upper back. Behind and in front of me were Sam and his family, barrelling me in a direction I didn't want to go.

'We have to turn back,' I blurted out suddenly. 'She needs to sleep.'

'The crying doesn't bother us,' said Bridget, lobbing me a cordial invitation to retract my statement.

'It bothers me a lot,' I said, dropping my proverbial tennis racket with a thud.

An awkward untangling ensued.

'Do you think I could grab my roll for the walk back?' I asked.

A tui called somewhere in the distance.

'Of course you can,' said Bridget, removing her backpack and unzipping it, the sound cutting through the quiet bush like a feller buncher.

'Amazing! Thanks!' I said, heart racing as I accepted my prize. 'See y'all back at the ranch!'

I was Southern now, and had quit blinking some time ago.

Sam and I ran through our repertoire of nursery rhymes on our way back to the car while Dee Dee continued to cry. I'd noted his silence during our parting. I knew on some level he believed we should have continued up the mountain in spite of our discomfort, even because of it. And I had an irresistible urge to convince him that he was wrong.

'*Down came the rain and washed poor Incy out . . .*'

For now, at least, we were united in song, but the air was heavy with the mutual realisation that we would forever be reconciling different ends of the emotional spectrum: Sam's family's 'Self-control is the goal' versus my family's 'Etiquette? Forgetiquette!'

'Could your mum have been more reluctant to give up that roll?' I asked, adopting an even tone.

'What do you mean?' he replied, denial a hallmark of his creed.

'Oh, please. They were disappointed in us for leaving. We're flakes now, according to them. Coupla no-good quitters.'

'They didn't say anything of the sort.'

'The silence was deafening. I mean, *Just say it!* They're like . . . silent assassins! Silence is violence!'

I was losing him. If I was going to change his core emotional values before we reached the car park, I needed to get organised.

'Sorry,' I said. 'I'm just upset because I don't think we did anything wrong by leaving.'

'Neither do I. We made exactly the right decision for us.'

'And you believe that with every bone in your body? Swear on Dee Dee's life.'

'Jesus. Okay, maybe there's a small part of me that thinks we should have stayed, but the practical reasons for turning back far outweighed it.'

'So you admit it then!' I said, energised by a faint whiff of victory.

'Admit what? That a bit of persistence and grit can be okay sometimes?'

'I have both in spades, mate. Do you realise where I am right now? On a bushwalk. That I stayed on. For a while.'

'Why do you care if they were disappointed in us for leaving? It shouldn't matter what they think.'

'It matters what *you* think. And the reason it matters is strapped to your chest.'

We walked on in silence, my triumphant last line dissipating in the air like fireworks.

'I want Dee Dee to grow up knowing how to trust and value her feelings,' I said, filled with the generosity afforded by certain victory.

'So do I, but I also want her to have resolve and perseverance.'

'Absolutely. If it's for something she cares about. Not because she's trying to live up to our expectations.'

'But wouldn't you call that an expectation?'

Later that afternoon, Bridget took Dee Dee to the water's edge. I followed and took some photos with my phone. They cut a striking tableau, Bridget striding in a straw hat and black swimsuit to the lake she knew. Dee Dee on her hip, uncertain, toothless and nude.

Bridget lowered her onto the wet sand. Dee Dee closed her eyes and swayed a little, relinquishing her full weight onto her grandmother's forearm. As I was returning to the house, I caught a peripheral blur of snarling grey. The large dog from a few houses over came loping across the bank towards Dee Dee, incensed by the audacity of her plumpness and size. Unflinching, Bridget swung her grandchild onto her hip and angled her body away from the animal. The dog barked loudly and Bridget's voice got low, her body strong and still until the dog turned back. Protecting ours.

DEATH TO BIRTH SHAME

When Evie described her un-medicated home birth as the most beautiful experience of her life, my first thought was 'ew.' Birth began with a mucus plug and things got more disgusting from there. But it was *the way* she said it that irked me most of all. Her peaceful smile and unabashed use of the word 'beautiful'. Her long, undone curls cascading past her breasts, just so. Evie had birthed her baby without needing medical intervention. She was the epitome of woman and I was not, and she was being so goddam nice about it, it made me sick.

On the scale of traumatic births Dee Dee's was reasonably mild (Syntocinon–fetal distress–episiotomy–vacuum–everyone basically fine), but the emotional impact was off the chart. I blamed myself for the induction and the danger it caused her. Had I not been so anxious, she would have glided to safety on a morning dew drop, my body doing what it was designed to do, i.e. opening resplendently like a water lily in bloom. At least that's what a lot of the non-medicalised birth books said. Instead, my body became something Dee Dee needed to be rescued from, a broken elevator in a bad action movie, the trapped young starlet's oxygen supply running out just as the doors were prised open and she was pulled to safety.

My second pregnancy unlocked everything I was too busy and overwhelmed to process during the first eighteen months of parenthood: my lack of faith in my body's ability to keep my baby safe, my fury at the medical system for fuelling my fear, my hurt over the Evies of the world for making me feel like a failure and the depth of unkindness I had towards myself.

In an attempt to ease my anxiety, Evie left a book about hypnobirthing on my doorstep, which she believed had greatly attributed to her beautiful birth. A chubby baby smiled over a misty pink background, the words 'natural' and 'birth' emblazoned across its forehead. I would have preferred a flaming bag of dog shit, but I didn't know Evie well enough to tell her that at the time.

The crux of hypnobirth is that through positive affirmations, breathing and visualisation, the vast majority of women can give birth un-medicated and with relative ease. I'd learned a little about it during my first pregnancy and blamed it almost entirely for how crap I felt over how the birth had turned out. The big idea is that women are in charge of the outcome of their birth—the flip side of that being the sense of crushing failure if things don't go to plan. Hypno-birthing was a dangerous game, but I really, really wanted my body to open like a water lily in bloom. I placed the book on the bench and came back to it during Dee Dee's midday nap. The chubby baby beckoned me from a patch of warm, milky sunlight, and in I fell.

Straight out of the gate, I learned that I could have given birth without intervention if I had a stronger connection to my maternal instinct. 'Wow, fuck you, Evie,' I said aloud, thumbing ahead to the chapter on positive affirmations. They were fine, but the parts about how I'd failed the last time were intoxicating. I was seduced by the author almost immediately, by the way they knew my most secret fears and how to make me not afraid anymore.

Your desire to protect your child wasn't powerful enough, they whispered between the lines. *You weren't powerful enough.*

'Yes, I am selfish and weak,' I murmured, 'that's why my birth was a miserable medical experiment.'

It was an embarrassment to women everywhere, but now is your chance to redeem yourself. Embrace my teachings fully and without question … or else burn in the fires of birth shame for all eternity.

The book's front cover curled up at the edges, which Evie had explained was the result of some light summer rain damage. I imagined her dozing on a banana lounge as she was misted with rain, those pinkish hues rising and falling on her belly with each contented breath.

'Why can't I be more like Evie?' I asked Dee Dee one afternoon, who looked up from her sunscreen finger painting on the bathroom tiles. I was emptying the contents of the vanity on the hunt for my old curling wand. 'Ugh, why can't I be more serene? Ah! There you are, you stupid rod fuck!'

Sporting a head of tight curls that splintered at the ends, I researched hypnobirthing late into the night. I learned about the inner workings of labour and how, in most cases, a birthing woman's body was an astoundingly efficient system. Contractions were triggered by oxytocin, the body's natural source of heroin, which caused a domino effect of opioids that helped to relieve pain. Basically, the more loved up I could feel during labour, the more oxytocin

I would produce, the more effective and less painful my contractions would be. Conversely, fear was the enemy of labour and birth, slowing contractions and tautening the cervix, which could result in complications and excruciating pain. I discovered how hospitals could be disruptive environments for labour, with their operating tables, medicines and gleaming birth instruments—all signs pointing to the labouring woman requiring assistance to birth her baby, planting seeds of oxytocin-slowing doubt.

In the hospital waiting room for my 28-week check-up, I watched a video of a woman birthing her own baby next to a slide in her backyard. It was her sixth free birth, each one going off without a hitch. She delivered her third on a picnic rug alone in the woods in the middle of the night. Hospitals made her feel stressed; death by wolves or exposure, or wolves raising her baby as their own after she had died from exposure, apparently did not. I wanted to project the slide video on the waiting room wall so that everyone would finally know the truth: Birth was a cinch.

'You see?' I'd say as it was playing, my eyes shining beneath a film of tears. 'We don't need all this medical saddlery. We just have to believe!'

The obstetrician listened patiently to my concerns about hospitals planting seeds of oxytocin-slowing doubt, and assured me my feelings were valid. She suggested I see my GP for the remainder of my check-ups instead of coming to the hospital, if it made me more comfortable. She was the voice of reason, the paradoxical middle ground between 'natural' and medicalised birth. I felt the hiss of months of built-up tension start to leave my neck and shoulders.

The door opened to reveal the bristling head of an obstetrician from down the hall. 'She's going to need a caesarean,' he barked.

'He doesn't mean you, Ashe!' said my doctor. 'Let me just quickly deal with this.'

She went into the hallway and closed the door. I heard parts of their muffled conversation about the pregnant person who was last in my chair. 'Nuchal cord' and 'fetal growth restriction' were reeled off like items on a grocery list.

The World Health Organization reported that in 2017, around 295,000 women died from pregnancy and childbirth–related causes. Ninety-four per cent of these deaths occurred in low-resource settings, and most could have been prevented with better access to medical care. Every year, millions of babies die during their first week of life for the same reason. Access to quality health care was an immense privilege, but also a double-edged sword due to its built-in risk aversion, a system that couldn't help but spook healthy preggos who just needed to calm their cervix.

Evie's book classified Dee Dee's birth as a 'horror story', regardless of it being one that resulted in a live, healthy mother and baby. I was strongly encouraged to keep it to myself, so as to spare other pregnant people the distress of my experience. I wasn't so much as to think about it, lest I hinder my chances of achieving a 'positive story'—meaning a strictly un-medicated vaginal birth—the second time around. The book was vehemently against me accepting pain medication during labour and birth, and suggested that my choice to do so may have resulted in my firstborn suffering long-term feelings of abandonment.

Evie's book was not having the desired effect. My cervix was not calm. My cervix was incensed. I vowed to destroy the misty-coloured fascist rag, but not before proving this fundamental part of its teachings wrong: that Dee Dee's birth was a horror story, and one that I needed to forget.

I took my seventeen-month-old scream queen to an Italian chain restaurant for dinner. It was 4 p.m. I ordered a small pizza for her and fettuccine carbonara for myself. In the pregnant community, the meal is known as dunch. The place was staffed by sturdy-armed women. A waitress with high cheekbones and a raspy voice got a colouring book and pencils for Dee Dee. She asked me when I was due and I said around Christmas. Then she told me how her daughter-in-law tore so badly during the birth of her second child the doctor had to reattach her clitoris.

'Carbonara extra bacon bits?' said another waitress, who had arrived to deliver my order.

Evie's book and I could agree at last: some birth stories were better left unsaid in certain situations, like when you're talking to a heavily pregnant stranger near a bowl of ham. Though technically speaking, it still wasn't a horror story. As far as I was aware, the devil did not start speaking to the daughter-in-law through her clitoris. And surely the waitress would have mentioned it if after the procedure the obstetrician murdered everyone while wearing a full face of clown make-up. She didn't strike me as the type to sit on a secret like that.

Instead of avoiding birth horror stories, I decided it best to disprove their very existence, and figured the history of western medicalised birth to be the most obvious place to start. It was a useful exercise in that it helped give context to Dee Dee's birth. The better I understood how it came to be, the easier it was to accept, and the more relaxed my cervix and I became. *Take that, Evie*, I thought, clicking through to a blog on the disease-ridden maternity wards of nineteenth century Europe.

At 33 weeks, I booked an appointment with an acupuncturist. I lay on the bed with my eyes closed while Lucinda moved silently around the dim room, her soothing voice the only indication of the direction from which the next needle would come. She suggested I read *Spiritual Midwifery* by Ina May Gaskin, the unofficial manifesto for non-medicalised birth, because for the remainder of my pregnancy I should focus exclusively on 'positive birth stories'.

'Oops, you've just popped a needle out!' she said. 'Try not to furrow your brow, Ashe.'

'It's just that I'm more into birth in the Middle Ages at the moment,' I murmured.

'Oh? What's drawn you to that particular era?'

'The alleged horror.'

'That doesn't sound too relaxing!' she said. 'I'm just putting a needle in your neck, now. Breathing out. There we go.'

'Specifically what women were able to achieve in spite of it.'

'In spite of . . . the horror?'

'Allegedly. Most of the births were successful, despite society's indifference as to whether women lived or died. They're a testament to the strength of the female spirit.'

'That's lovely. Now if you can just roll gently to your side so I can work on your lower back, Ashe. You said you were having some pain? How have your bowel movements been?'

'Then you go back even further and there's Aristotle, who's considered this hero of the modern "natural" birth movement, but the reason he didn't want to intervene with birth is because he thought women should resume their natural state of passive obedience so as best to endure their reckoning. He was a foaming-at-the-mouth misogynist. He had a whole philosophy on women being mutilated males. When they birthed, I imagine they simply became instruments of his beloved nature. But birthing women have always been viewed as instruments of a higher power, whether it's nature or medicine or God. Giving birth to humans is so human and yet utterly dehumanising—isn't it fascinating? Sorry, did you ask me a question?'

'Oh just . . . bowel movements?'

'Yeah, very infrequent.'

In 2018 a statue of Dr J. Marion Sims was removed from New York City's Central Park to thunderous applause. He's known as the 'grandfather of gynaecology' (because that's not a creepy thing to say!) due to figuring out how to repair tears in the vaginal wall postpartum. He did so by performing experimental surgeries on enslaved African women in Alabama from 1845 to 1849 with no anaesthesia, even though it had been invented. These women were literally reduced to instruments of medicine. Sims recorded just three of their (slave) names: Lucy, Anarcha and Betsey. My cervix tore during Dee Dee's birth and the obstetrician used Sims's findings to repair it afterwards. I'm indebted to Lucy, Anarcha, Betsey and the other women who never had a say in helping me. I imagined them in that makeshift hospital in the backyard at night, when Sims had returned to the main house, and the things they might have whispered to each other in the dark.

By late November I was 36 weeks. The foam of the couch made my legs itch and the baby kicked wildly. Dee Dee had thrown up and I'd put the cushion covers in three buckets to soak, one in each. Even in their own apartments they looked crowded and miserable. It must have been 30 degrees in the living room. Dee Dee had bounced back from her illness and was building towers of canned goods in various places around the house, a thrilling and studious new game. I had two tabs open on my phone: 'How long cooked sausage good' and 'DIY air conditioner'. Sam was out. I flipped through Evie's book for old times' sake. The breathing exercises and visualisations still felt relevant. The preordained shame should I need or want medical intervention during the birth did not.

At my last appointment, the waiting room was flush with expectant mothers. A wisdom of pregnant people. The first-timers rubbed their bellies in quiet contemplation while the rest of us heaved ourselves after children we had prepared earlier. Some wore striped tube dresses that clung to their bellies, others wore hijabs and long flowing robes. Each of us would soon add a new section to the great tapestry of birth, some with actual stitches, but none whose story would live in the horror section. Romance, sure, or romantic comedy or drama. There might have been a romantic thriller in the making, but that would require a midwife to have been slowly poisoning one of us over several months with plans to steal the baby and assume our identity, which seemed unlikely. I'd decided Dee Dee's birth story was a romantic drama. It had twists and turns, laughter and tears. And rain! So much rain. It was basically *The Notebook*. At its heart was a woman who was scared to be a mother and the person who would make her not afraid anymore. The book on hypnobirthing, and fanatics as a rule, just lacked imagination when it came to good storytelling.

★

Frances June Mackenport arrived on Christmas Eve. The drive to the hospital was sun-dappled and quiet. People were off enjoying their summers. Preparation and luck had made for a reasonably comfortable labour. I was five centimetres dilated when we arrived. The midwives had us wait in the resuscitation room because it was the only one available. I leaned on a table amidst tubes and defibrillator pads, gazing up at a chart on protocol in the event of a cardiac arrest.

'They're fucking with us, surely,' said Sam.

We laughed and my uterus contracted. He counted down from twenty, like we'd practised.

'You can't be my five-centimetre,' said a midwife, entering the room, and later in the birthing suite: 'You're doing well now, but it's about to get a lot harder to cope with.'

Franny released her water Nickelodeon slime–style. I was on all fours and the midwife was examining my cervix like a mechanic under a car. It hit with such force it made an audible splat.

That's my girl, I remember thinking.

My mother arrived shortly after. She hung back mostly, watching her labouring child like a tourist at a church service. That is, until Franny decided it was showtime. The final stages happened so fast I stopped being able to see, hear or comprehend. The head was emerging, they were trying to tell me, but all I heard was static and madness. I wanted out of the room, off the bed, no, finished, cut to black.

'Hold her shoulder,' my mother was saying to Sam, at the forefront now, pinning my left side with the length of her body. She knew the force of my resistance, which in full, animalistic flight was powerful enough to take on three adults, a birth and all sense of reason.

'Listen, Ashe,' she was saying. 'Listen, listen.'

I found her voice like a rope in a snowstorm. It led me back to my body, to the bed, and Sam, and the midwife, and the passer-by who'd been helping to restrain me.

Moments later, Franny arrived, and we all cried together.

TWO UNDER TWO IS THE LONELIEST NUMBER

'Hiii, you've rung the postnatal depression helpline, you're speaking with Lucyy, how can I help youu?' Lucy's sympathy dripped gently through the receiver.

'Hi, I'm Ashe. I have a toddler and a newborn and um . . . I'm in hell.'

'Mmmm, lots of big changes going on at your place thennn.'

'Lots more eating shit than I was expecting.'

'Ohhhhh no. That doesn't sound too good.'

'It's violently degrading.'

'That must be tough, to view your life in that way.'

'I haven't slept in three weeks and there's a river of

diarrhoea down the hallway. I'd say it's a pretty objective view of my life. Are you a mum, Lucy?'

'Yes, but I'm more interested in talking about *your* experience.'

'Perfect. You're eating shit too then. I guess what I'm wondering is, how much shit can a person eat before it leaves a permanent shit stain on their sense of self-worth?'

'Mmmm. What an interesting question, Ashe. Do you have people in your life who offer you the support you need?'

'I guess. I don't know. I feel better just from saying that out loud to you now, actually. Thanks for listening.'

'Ashe, I'd like to send you some information on postna—'

I hung up, figuring it was best to free up the line. There was probably a woman on hold who was convinced her baby was the devil. Also, Dee Dee was about to insert a crayon into Franny's fontanel.

'Dee Dee, I won't let you do that,' I said, removing the crayon from her hand. 'That would hurt Franny.'

I peered at the pulsing soft spot on top of my baby's bald head, one of the membranous gaps between the bones of her skull. They would close over the coming months and years as her mind became her own. At six weeks old, her dissatisfactions and desires were expressed with loud continuous cries. She couldn't keep a single one of her thoughts private. It made sense that I could see her brain.

I ran a bath for Dee Dee and devised a cleaning strategy for the hall, the result of her trying to run away from her own diarrhoea, an instinct I could relate to but never had the courage to act on.

Miraculously, after cleaning the hall and bathing the toddler and feeding the baby and the toddler and cleaning the kitchen and the baby and the toddler, there was a moment when both my children were sleeping. I took the opportunity to open the doors and windows, make myself a cup of tea and consider the pool of wet shit that was my life. The conversation with Lucy had done little to satisfy my urge to complain about it. It was insatiable. I wanted to unpack every hardship of life with two children under two in excruciating detail. I wanted to wrap myself in my sour-smelling dressing-gown and expound negativity over mugs of cold coffee—but with who? I mean, during business hours, when my partner was at work? Most of my parent friends were luxuriating in the celestial city that is only-child parenting. They couldn't possibly understand what I was going through. One of the cruellest tricks of parenthood is that we only find out how good we had it when it's too late. I imagine inmates of maximum-security prisons can relate upon being moved to solitary confinement. So the pulled pork on taco Tuesday in the main jail was mostly tanbark—at least you knew it was Tuesday. The life of a typical parent of one was scheduled around a single nap routine, while dinner time consisted simply of plonking a bowl of spaghetti in front of their kid and a straw in a bottle of pinot grigio. Their complaints about teething and daycare centres being closed on public holidays now made me laugh for minutes at a time, loudly, and mere inches from their faces. Single parents and parents of kids with special needs would no doubt do the same to me, not to mention be well within their rights to punch me squarely in the tit. I could complain to child-free friends to a point, but couldn't really let them have it for fear of cancelling the human race.

I didn't want to admit that I was struggling. After Dee Dee's birth, I forgave myself (kind of) for feeling lost and overwhelmed. The job was new and challenging so it made (slightly) more sense to me to ask for help. Then, around Dee Dee's first birthday, my uterus lured me into wanting another baby with its hypnotic sibling song. Franny arrived a year later, rendering me doubly in need of support, but doubly resistant to seek it. I rated high on postnatal depression quizzes, but took them privately and shared the results with no one. I couldn't shake the feeling that admitting depression would mean admitting I was incapable of caring for my kids. I called Lucy because I needed help and she knew it. 'I'm not coping' were the words I couldn't say. Instead I told her she was eating shit in an attempt to avoid feeling like a failure. I became a crocodile mum: isolated, aggressive and leathery to the touch.

In my experience, a dream birth did not equate to a dream fourth trimester. Franny's arrival read like a storybook. She was born on Christmas Eve in relatively uncomplicated fashion. When I awoke the following morning, I rose from my hospital bed with the excitement of a six-year-old, except less sprightly and more post-birthy. Franny was asleep in her capsule, wrapped in a honey-coloured blanket. She looked like a freshly baked loaf of sourdough. Her tiny ribcage rose and fell with each rapid breath. I couldn't process the volume of wonder that lay before me.

Once home, family members trickled by through the day with offerings of cold cuts and Christmas pudding, which we ate on the living room floor, marvelling at our perfect new addition asleep in the Moses basket.

Twenty-month-old Dee Dee was filled with a furious love for her baby sister. When we arrived home, she tore out of the bedroom and emptied the contents of several kitchen drawers. Moments later she appeared, beaming, with an armful of empty baby bottles, which she dumped squarely on Franny's head.

Dee Dee had always twirled her hair to fall asleep, a self-soothing technique likened to thumb-sucking, but after Franny was born, twirling no longer had the desired effect. Instead, she began pulling it out in clumps. I'd discover them on her mattress in the morning, bleary-eyed from a 45-minute sleep between feeds, unsure if I was awake or having a vivid Freudian nightmare.

'If you tell anyone about the h-a-i-r, I'll file for d-i-v-o-r-c-e,' I said to Sam over breakfast one morning.

We had taken to spelling out the words 'hair', 'pulling' and 'divorce', or swapping them for toddler-proof ones such as 'follicle', 'removal' and 'conscious uncoupling'. The internet had advised us to draw as little of Dee Dee's attention to her hair as possible.

'I won't,' he said, peering at the newest bald patch on Dee Dee's head. 'What if my parents notice it at dinner tomorrow night?'

'They won't. I'm going to stay home with the girls. I'm not up for it.'

'Okay,' he said. 'Mum's really keen to visit, though. When do you think would be a good time for her to do that?'

'Hmm, I guess never?'

He sighed and blew a raspberry on Dee Dee's neck. She squealed with delirium.

'Your mum's been calling me too. What if you made visiting hours from ten to midday on a particular day of the week or something? Get it all out of the way in one go.'

I shuddered. 'Like in prison?'

'Why not?' he asked.

'Because I'd be a sitting duck! I'm not agreeing to being strung up naked for two hours a week so I can be f-u-c-k-e-d by our mums.'

'Wait, what?'

'It would feel extremely violating to me. I'll have them around the moment I can stand the thought of one of them having any kind of opinion about anything. Even ones they keep to themselves. Ugh, especially those.' I bit savagely into a piece of cold toast.

'Alright,' he said. 'Are you okay?'

'Fucking fantastic.'

'Fuck! Fuck! Fuck!' said Dee Dee.

I went to a bar for a friend's birthday, figuring it would be a welcome distraction from the family grind. I arrived early, having fantasised about sitting on a bar stool with a book and a glass of wine for a solid year.

'A pinot noir, please,' I said to the bartender over my faded copy of *The Great Gatsby*. I'd bought it from a second-hand bookstore one rainy afternoon before Dee Dee was born.

'Sorry?' The bartender leaned his ear towards me.

My stomach lurched. Oh God, did I say that wrong? Did my mouth make words or just sounds? I haven't read a word of this book since year eleven and he knows it. It's a prop in a pantomime, where I play the part of a woman who leaves her house at night with friends to meet and interests of her own, as demonstrated by her classic novel, which might as well be filled with blank pages, emptier than one of Gatsby's parties. He was the Tobey Maguire one, right?

'A PINOT NOIR?' I shouted, in the silence between songs.

He laughed and said, 'Okee dokee.'

I wanted to go home or, better yet, eat dessert at the Italian restaurant I'd spotted a few doors down then go home. I was about to cancel my drink order when Nina appeared beside me.

'Hi, Mumma,' she said and kissed me on the cheek. 'Catching up on some reading, are we?'

Nina. Birthday. Nina's birthday. That's why I'm here. 'Hi,' I said. 'Happy birthday! I've read this.'

'Thanks for coming,' she said.

'Wouldn't miss it for the world.'

Some more child-free people arrived and the group moved to a table in the courtyard. The conversation catapulted from exhibitions I hadn't heard of to bands I didn't know. Two people thought it was okay to share with me that they thought I looked tired. I kept quiet mostly, giving my own leg an occasional reassuring squeeze under the table. I was seated next to one of Nina's friends, a woman ten years younger than me who was a film student at RMIT.

'Have you seen *Loveless* yet?' she asked. 'I saw it this afternoon, it's stunning.'

'I don't know what that is,' I said.

'It's a Russian film about marital collapse and the state of modern Russia.'

'Maybe I'll catch the Pixar remake.'

She laughed a luminous, carefree laugh that made me wish her unwell. 'How many kids do you have again?'

'Two.'

'Wow, you look great for having two kids.'

I drained the last of my glass. 'Goodnight, everybody.'

That night, Franny woke for feeds at eleven, three and five. Two roadwork labourers struck up a loud conversation outside our house at six, at which point I went into the street in my pyjamas.

'Can you please keep it down?' I yelled over the fence. 'THANK YOU! THANKS SO MUCH!'

'Sorry to wake you,' one of the men replied. 'You okay, darlin'?'

Caught off guard by his kind eyes and ability to call me darlin' without causing offence, my eyes filled with tears. 'No,' I whispered.

When I got back inside Dee Dee was sitting puffy-eyed on the edge of our bed wearing a nappy and Ninja Turtles t-shirt, her feathery auburn hair brushed into an adorable comb-over.

'Mummy!' she said, swinging her legs. 'Nice sweep?'

Sam dressed her before he left for work, his way of gently suggesting that we leave the house at some point during the day. I had taken to staying indoors, despite the fact that it was the middle of summer and we didn't have air conditioning. Franny didn't like being in the pram or the car seat, and let me know by screaming at a level disproportionate to her seven-kilogram body weight. Leaving the house felt like going through a tunnel of screeching bats. Once on the other side, it was no picnic. Chasing after a toddler while breastfeeding was hard enough at home, let alone in an unfenced park by a main road.

The logistical challenges of going out were compounded by my sadness and vice versa. I believed I was doing a terrible job, and the belief seemed to actualise whenever I left the house. On a particularly colourful journey to the library, I screamed at Dee Dee to

'GET IN THE PRAM NOW' and a little old woman came out of her house to fold her arms and glare at me like a mafia boss, letting me know she had her eye on me. Once a man yelled at me from his car because I didn't cross at the pedestrian crossing. When I told him where he could shove his suggestion, he followed us for a block, berating me about what kind of mother I was. Even when I wasn't being harassed by strangers on the street it was chaos. Dee Dee wandered behind cafe counters and broke water glasses on the floor. Franny screamed like she was on fire. I felt powerless, like a chip packet caught in the bristles of an automatic car wash. It was safer to stay indoors, in our darkened sauna, blinds closed, *Hey Duggee* on loop.

'Been getting out and about?' my mother asked one afternoon, cooling herself by the desk fan in the living room.

'About as much as to be expected,' I replied, fighting the urge to flip the coffee table and scream, 'How could you accuse me of failing as a mother?!'

'What can I do?' she asked.

'Nothing,' I said. 'I'm meeting a friend for a playdate.'

She sighed, knowing full well it was a lie. My plan for the rest of the day was to microwave cheese on bread and eat it over the sink.

'Cancel the playdate,' she said. 'I'll take Dee Dee for a walk. Franny's asleep. Take a nap.'

'No, really, it's fine,' I said, and sank deeper into my wallow.

My first successful outing was to the park at the end of our street. I pushed through Franny's screams with the aid of Joni Mitchell and noise-cancelling headphones, and by the time we arrived she was sound asleep. Dee Dee stumbled onto the playground like a newborn foal, squinting in the natural light. I sat on a bench and watched her play, my sense of accomplishment rising steadily with my vitamin D levels. It must have been fifteen minutes before Franny stirred in the pram.

'She's awake!' I yelled across the playground. 'Abort mission! Abort! Abort!'

I roared the pram over to where Dee Dee was playing and hurled her into the moving vehicle. By the time we got home Franny was asleep again, the new extension of my bursting, buried heart.

VAGINA MOMOLOGUE

It's Saturday morning and I am standing in the bathroom with a hand mirror. Sam is in the backyard with Dee Dee. I can hear him teaching her how to water the plants. Her silence implies about as much focus as a two-year-old can muster. She's listening with her whole body. I'm about to look at my vagina for the first time in a long time—but that's not right. Vagina is the name for the inside part. I'd need something more high-tech than a hand mirror to do that. I'm referring to my *vulva* and *perineum*. Why are those words hard to say? Surely it's relevant to the issue at hand. I fear my episiotomy scar has made them appear crooked and ugly, like Hatchet-Face from the movie

Cry-Baby. I remind myself that Hatchet never thought there was anything wrong with her face. According to her, it just had character.

In 2008, I declined an artist's request to sculpt my vulva. His name was Greg Taylor, and his work *Cunts and other conversations* went on to be displayed at Mona. My vulva could have been famous. I didn't mind the name. In Latin, 'vagina' literally translates to 'sheath or scabbard', i.e. a case for a knife or sword. Cunt is only marginally more offensive than that. I interviewed Taylor for a web series that now lives on a hard drive somewhere in the northern suburbs. We were in his studio, surrounded by rows of life-size vulvas, every hair follicle and skin fold sculpted meticulously out of clay. During our conversation, I had done an okay job of pretending to be comfortable with the work. *This wall of vividly naturalistic female genitalia doesn't make me feel queasy at all!* I told myself. *This is important work. And besides, the queasier I am, the more important it is!* When Greg showed me his sculpture of a vulva belonging to a 70-year-old woman who had given birth to nine children, I was genuinely moved, so much so that I left any cats having nine lives jokes on the low-hanging branches where they belonged. But I also felt like I might faint. When he asked if I would consider posing for him, I remember laughing too loudly and the feeling of heat rising up my neck. Not if you landed me an internship at *RUSSH* magazine and a date with Julian Casablancas, I thought, thanking him and pretending I'd consider it.

In theory, Taylor's offer should have been a win-win. As an abandoned middle child and ex-drama student, attention filled the cavernous hole at the core of my being, or at least tickled the sides. I loved a spotlight. I volunteered as a hair model for countless apprentices-in-training, and would clear a weekend to pose in a laneway for a friend of a friend's uni photography assignment. I declined to be sculpted for *Cunts* because I thought vulvas were gross, and mine in particular. Faced with a room of art intended to encourage me to believe otherwise, I held on to it as fact.

'Fwowa,' says Dee Dee from the garden.

'That's right,' says Sam. 'Flower.'

I inhale sharply, momentarily triggered by the countless flower time-lapses I'd been exposed to while preparing for birth. They emerge from my memory like spiders from a cave. *Just imagine your vagina as a rose in bloom*, the natural-birth books said, written by people apparently not up to date with the modern definition of rosebudding.

Pre-kids, I'd established an amicable working relationship with my vulva and vagina. We were colleagues. They helped me get off, and in turn, I provided them with hygiene and healthcare benefits. I had no interest in knowing them outside of work hours. *If it ain't broke!* I might have explained at business events for people and vulvas, my palms sweating from the grossly discriminatory truth of the matter: I didn't like how they looked or smelled. Sexual partners were given the user manual during orientation, and improvisation was strongly discouraged. I employed strict company policies around oral sex, for instance, which was to take place only immediately after a shower, for no longer than a few minutes, cloaked in total darkness.

Post-kids, I took great comfort in letting go of myself as a sexual being. I didn't miss the act of sex, in the same way I imagine a nun isn't running around the convent horny out of her mind. I had a clear and noble purpose: to facilitate the lives of my children. My devotion to the cause would be all the motivation I needed. Or whatever the stuff was that kept me carrying and coaxing them to baby osteo appointments while my back privately ached. In place of the pursuit of any desires of my own, I imagined I would simply fashion a nest of blankets on the living room floor and chain myself to the radiator, where my children could suckle at my teat until I was nothing but an honourable husk, misty-eyed with joy.

Recently, I found a lacy black slip in my drawer and

yelled, 'Dick!' the way someone with dementia might say, 'Roses!' at the touch of their gardening gloves and the fleeting memory of a life before.

Sex had become something I 'put out' rather than enjoyed. My vagina had never felt less like my own. It was an event space. It hosted intercourse, rites of passage and various medical agendas. Bookings had slowed considerably in recent years. The garden was overgrown and the letterbox was stuffed with electricity bills, threatening to disconnect.

On Tuesdays we went to the library for Rhyme Time. Local parents and I would sit on the floor of the children's book section and sing nursery rhymes to our bedrooled. Afterwards, we would murmur our names and babies' ages and forget them almost immediately, as our children gained a million neural connections with every passing second. In the park across the street, I watched a pregnant parent wandering after two small children who were kicking a ball. She wore faded khaki shorts, a sunhat and t-shirt in a similar smear of nothing.

I decided to pursue an interest outside of parenting. After two years of murmuring in washed out cottons, I felt something obnoxiously loud was in order. I found a Broadway dance class on Saturdays at 8 a.m. featuring routines to the *Grease* soundtrack and Tina Turner, the musical.[1] The instructor was a man named Brendy Ford, a drill sergeant in heels who yelled things like, 'Who cares if you fuck up, just keep dancing!'

A section of the warm-up was languidly sexual, and sometimes involved rolling on the floor to Rizzo's 'There Are Worse Things I Could Do' or stretching to 'We Are the Champions' from Queen, the musical.[2] We lay on our backs with our legs spread in the air for the chorus, holding the pose for some time, the studio-length mirror reflecting row after row of triumphant Vs.

'Deedeebur,' says Dee Dee. She thinks ladybirds are called 'Dee Dee birds'. The day she learns the truth, a part of me will surely die.

My eyes are closed as I lower the mirror. I'm walking in darkness towards the sound of soft piano music. It's stirring and familiar, with an unmistakable note of defiance. A drum sounds from deep in my chest and electric guitar surges through my veins as the mirror reaches my crotch. I open my eyes at Freddie's soaring chorus and listen with my whole body.

---

1 *TINA: The Tina Turner Musical*

2 *We Will Rock You, The Musical* by Queen and Ben Elton

PARENTHOOD IS A KICK-ON

There's a moment at a play centre when you know you've stayed too long. It's usually around midday, when the number of patrons thins due to most of them going home for their afternoon nap. The same five songs lurch and skip from a portable speaker with flashing lights. The lyrics are about slides and jumping in ball pits, in case you had forgotten where you were. Shoeless, you sip your third greyish latte and, from a colourful plastic chair, take in your surroundings for the first time in several hours. You hear the echo of your one-year-old and trace the sound to the top of a tube slide for the over-threes, while along a trail of odd shoes and costume parts an elderly woman smiles warmly at you, a memory of sharing with her the intricate details of your nipple thrush settling over you like mist.

In my twenties, I frequented a 24-hour club called Revolver. Around midday, as the drugs wore off, I'd squint at the daylight through the puckered venetian blinds. I'd scan the crowd for the friends I arrived with, then look down at the floor-length leather coat I'd been using as a blanket, tracing it to the stranger sitting next to me. He may have had a neck beard and a passion for crystals, but his interests were irrelevant. He was someone I'd gravitated towards in a drug-fuelled haze, led by a subconscious hunger for connection. We'd shared our darkest fears and most private memories, at one point mistaking loneliness for love, which was evident by the beer can ring on my finger, the last remaining memento of our commitment ceremony in the toilets after a Slurpee straw of MDMA.

Revolver was located above several shops on a main street in an affluent inner-city suburb. Once I'd gathered as many of my possessions as I could find, or remember having brought with me in the first place, I'd stumble down the steps and emerge onto the bustling shopping strip like a newborn ghoul. Standing along the displays of fresh produce outside the organic greengrocers would be the line of Revolver hopefuls, many of whom would be rejected either because they were too inebriated or the club was at capacity.

I was turned away from a play centre one rainy winter's morning. On the back of a largely sleepless night and morning of screaming tantrums, I barely noticed the cluster of disorientated parents and wailing children bumping into one another on the street. Inside, we were greeted by a woman with a clipboard.

'What name's the booking under?' she asked, clicking her pen.

Franny slid from my hip down the side of my body with the urgency of a firefighter.

'I don't have one,' I said. 'I didn't know I needed to book.'

'We've changed our policy on that,' she said, smiling fiercely. 'I posted it on our Facebook page and Instagram.'

Dee Dee and Franny rattled the gate to the crowded play area, whimpering gently.

'I don't follow play centres on social media,' I said, feeling a tightness in my jaw. 'Nobody does. That's not a thing.'

You think you're so important with your clipboard and your lice-plagued costume box, I wanted to say. *I cleaned a smashed jar of anchovies at five thirty this morning, lady. IN OIL. You don't know what I've been through to get here. YOU DON'T KNOW WHAT I'VE SEEN.*

The woman maintained eye contact as her smile pulled further across her face, knowing if she let her eyes drop to the children's height all would be lost. This was about the big picture, not individual sob stories. Her stance was for the good of the children already inside.

I envisioned headbutting her.

'Hiiiiiiiiiiiiiiii,' came a voice from behind me. It was Marla, one of the parents from daycare.

'Hi, Marla. How are you?'

'We're great. Cornelius is keeping me busy, busy, busy!'

I sighed. She needed this. 'How's he going?'

'Oh, you know, he's being Cornelius! Courageous, inquisitive, just such a typical Sagittarius. From day one he's been fascinated with the world. That's why he was crawling and walking before all the other babies, do you remember? He couldn't wait to start exploring! The booking's under "Cornelius plus Mummy", thanks, Kerri. Are you coming in, Ashe?'

'We were just leaving, but you guys have fun. Make sure you explore the wigs,' I said, resisting the urge to scratch my scalp at the mention of the word. 'It's such a great age for imaginary play.'

'Tell me about it. Bye-bye, girls, watch fingers.' She closed the gate firmly behind her.

The first time I met Marla was in the park near my house. Cornelius was three months old and didn't sleep for more than 40 minutes at a stretch.

She looked like she'd spent her life in a windowless room, an image suggested by her watery eyes and the thinness of her skin. The day was overcast and a strong wind distorted her voice, making her sound far away. Without knowing my name, she shared her fears for her son's health and her own ability to love him.

I saw Marla again a month later at a cafe. With her ruddy cheeks and running tights, she was barely recognisable. Cornelius had started sleeping longer through the night, she explained. He'd had an extreme case of reflux, but had since come through the other side of it. She made no other reference to our first meeting. We exchanged some details regarding local roadworks and the library's school holiday program then continued on our separate paths.

Outside the play centre it was cold and desolate. An empty Tiny Teddies packet tumbled along the pavement, which was wet with rain and the tears of children. I called my sister Georgie and told her the situation. She was still an hour away, which was commendable given she was travelling with a five-week-old baby and a two-year-old. She deserved to have a statue erected in her honour in the city square, and nothing less.

A week earlier, she had her maternal child health appointment in her front yard while her two-year-old was locked in the house. She'd stepped outside with her new baby in the carrier and pictured her keys on the counter just as her toddler slammed the front door. Luckily, our sister Sam had a spare key and was available to drop it off. Unluckily, the nurse arrived before she did, and discovered Georgie breastfeeding in a bush while holding a clip of *Peppa Pig* against the living room window. For weeks afterwards, midwives popped over unexpectedly to see how she was doing, the lockout episode apparently having qualified her as a mother requiring extra support, or surveillance, depending on how you looked at it.

Like partying, early parenthood was a world within a world, with its own set of entirely uncivilised customs. In the former, people snorted mystery powder from public toilet lids. In the latter, they made porridge with breast milk and used the word 'poonami' as casually as 'stapler' or 'hat'. Visitors to either place often had the audacity to show up empty-handed, and settle in for the foreseeable future with the last drop of their host's wine or milk for their cup of tea. Sleeplessness was a recurring theme across the board, as were unusual mashups of regular feelings such as 'crowded isolation', 'sexless passion' and 'functional delirium'.

The play centre was in a strange suburb, the middle point between my place and Georgie's. I told her I'd investigate the reserve across the street and report back as to whether it might contain our toddlers for a while. There could be a playground there, or hoodie someone had left in the stands of the football ground. *We could have our own dress-ups, Marla.* I didn't have an umbrella, but that was okay. It had stopped raining by then. Things were looking up.

Getting denied entry to Revolver was a problem that was easily solved. There was a 24-hour bottle shop a block away. All you needed was alcohol and you could keep partying. A park. Maybe the courtyard of a share house of a friend of a friend. The goal was just to avoid going home at all costs, a prospect as appealing as death.

Georgie and I met at another play centre a suburb away. The walls inside were painted with cartoon smiling elephants with bulging eyes. They looked happy, but manic, like they were trapped forever on a rollercoaster. Or at least for the next eighteen years. Georgie's baby was asleep in the pram and our toddlers were contained on the jumping castle.

'You're a goddamn hero for making it here,' I said.

'Are you kidding? The thought of being trapped in the house all day,' she shuddered and took a sip from her sweet, milky coffee. 'This is bliss.'

VIOLET

'And another thing, Noreen,' I'd say, with one foot on my chair in a commanding lunge. 'Sam's great-grandmother singlehandedly kept a family of eight from starving during the Depression era. Where's her claim to her great-great-grandchild? Dee Dee wouldn't be here if it wasn't for Violet.'

'Women are the backbone of a family,' Noreen would declare, thumping her desk, and in doing so releasing the ballpoint pen that had been slowly suffocating in her fist. 'They're not the face. Where's the modesty in a woman scrawlin' her own name on her children?'

'I believe what you're referring to is "invisible labour", Noreen. Look it up.'

Violet Beale was born in Macetown, a mining settlement in the New Zealand snowfields, with no roads in or out at the time. Thirty years prior, the Mace brothers came across the site almost simultaneously with the Beale Brothers. Had the wind changed even slightly, Violet might have been born in Bealetown.

She was a dark-haired Irishwoman measuring well under five feet, only slightly shorter than her husband Jack, a barber and gambler with an impeccable handlebar moustache. Violet was a seamstress and a businesswoman. The diminutive pair provided services to miners in the area. When their business was destroyed in a fire the family moved to Christchurch, where Jack's gambling got worse and the Great Depression deepened. They survived on Violet's seamstress work and the wage her eldest daughter Frances made at the local department store. Her boss had a habit of scheduling after-hours meetings, so that he and Frances could be alone.

One night, Frances returned home later than usual. Violet could see she'd been crying and asked her what was the matter, though she had suspected the answer some time ago.

'I can't keep working there,' whispered Frances. 'It's Mr Michaels. He . . .'

Violet took her daughter's trembling hands in her own. 'People who can't work have two broken legs. Off to bed with you.'

Violet was a 'mama bear' in a truer sense than the way it's applied today. Her job was to effectively allocate resources to ensure the collective survival of her young. If a mother bear in the wild can't find enough to eat, she will typically kill and consume her cubs. Without enough nourishment to produce the milk required to nurse them, her cubs will surely die, and so they become a resource the mother bear can't afford to waste. The meat will restore her strength and fertility, which will increase the likelihood of successfully rearing cubs in the future.

Frances would go on to marry a larger-than-life Scotsman by the name of Mackisack, whose first name also happened to be Francis. They adored one another. She changed her name to 'Sally' to accommodate him, which was a pattern of theirs. She was a borderline agoraphobe with a rich inner life, gentle and very bright. She might have been well-suited to a career in academia, had it been an option for her at the time.

'Violet and Sally had eyes just like yours,' I'd say to Dee Dee, who would have just solved a Rubik's cube from the toy box in Noreen's office, causing Noreen to have fallen heavily from her chair.

'The colour of moss and wood,' I'd continue, helping Noreen from the floor. 'Gleaming with secrets.'

'You share DNA with your ancestors,' Noreen would say, vehemently brushing lint from her clothes.

'That means something. Mackenport doesn't. Son of Enport? I mean really.'

'Maybe it means "Son of no one". Ever think of that?'

'Not that it matters. The Mackenport tree will be cut down just as soon as it sprouted. Marriage and children will be sure of it.'

'If it comes to that, at least it'll be theirs to cut,' I'd say, flicking on the kettle in the kitchenette, Noreen and I glaring at each other through the steam.

THE SECRET TO A HAPPY MARRIAGE

I found a photo of my parents on a Greek island in the 1970s. They're standing in a line of people linking arms under a waterfall. My mother is screaming in overalls and my father is laughing with his head thrown back. They're young and tanned. The photo was in a box in the spare room at my grandparents' house in the Dandenong Ranges. I placed it on the carpet, peering into it from a crouching position, a faded portal to another dimension. It defied everything I knew about my parents' relationship.

Sam was helping my grandmother in the kitchen. I could hear her telling him to keep the screen door closed so as not to let a cat inside.

'I don't know whose cat it is,' she was saying, 'but he has an unpleasant nature. I only feed him on the porch. He's not allowed in the house.'

'Where's the big ginger cat?' asked Sam.

'I had him put down. Stomach tumour. The owners weren't going to bother.'

'I'm sorry to hear it, Shirl.'

'We were madly in love right to the end,' she sighed. 'Oh well.'

Sam and I hadn't spoken in the car on the way up. In the morning, we'd fought at the market over the shopping list. He hadn't received my text message containing it and I'd rolled my eyes when he informed me of this fact. He snapped that it wasn't his fault and I seethed that he took it so seriously. Franny cried because she wanted a banana. Dee Dee threw herself on the ground because she knew we were arguing. Sam picked her up and carried her off. People stared. Franny cried more. I attempted to peel the banana with shaking hands.

How could you do this to me? thought Sam and I in perfect *Freaky Friday* unison.

'Does the baby want some honey melon?' boomed a well-meaning fruiterer.

I pretended not to hear, just wanting to disappear. I managed to pierce the skin of the banana. Franny continued to cry.

'DOES THE BABY WANT SOME HONEY MELON?'

'NO THANKS!' I screamed wildly.

I waited for Sam at the entrance to the car park and an old couple shuffled past holding hands. I figured they must have put up with a lot of shit.

There was a loud tapping on the spare room window. I shrieked. It was my grandfather in his electric wheelchair, walking stick in hand. He was making the journey from his bedroom to the kitchen, via the path that ran along the outside of the house. It was an alternative solution to replacing their indoor staircase with a ramp. Or to my grandmother dragging him from room to room on a sheet of heavy-duty plastic. She was adamant it would be a viable transport solution, if she could just find the right material.

My grandfather has advanced Parkinson's, which means his central nervous system has become a Persian rug dealer: it's been threatening to close for a decade. The disease makes his body indifferent to directions from his brain, which is a shame—for him, mostly, but also for us. He has things to say. He just can't always rely on his body to say them. During visits, we're robbed of several laughs as a result.

I went downstairs.

Franny was asleep in the car capsule and Dee Dee was playing with a stuffed polyester pig that was bigger than her. My grandmother had bought it from a flea market.

'I just thought it had X factor—don't you?' she was saying.

'In spades,' Sam agreed.

I slid my arm around his waist.

'We're going to need a bigger car to get that thing home.'

'Worth it if you ask me,' said Sam, winking. A flicker of love.

The wood-panelled walls were adorned with my grandfather's paintings: impressionistic landscapes and bowls of fruit, along with several Fauvist nudes of my grandmother. He was a baker all his life, and taught himself to paint during his retirement. His work suited the dark velvet furniture and jewel-toned vases, and the pink flowers that floated in a platter of water on the coffee table.

'Kim gave me the idea,' my grandmother explained. 'It makes me think of a gorgeous Moroccan brothel. Okay, who's ready to eat?'

I wondered if experimentation was the secret to a lasting marriage. It sounded like the tagline for a range of sex toys founded by an elderly couple in matching kaftans, but I stored it away regardless. I often found myself searching for relationship clues at my grandparents' house. After 65 years of marriage they still seemed to thoroughly enjoy each other's company. My grandfather had made my grandmother breakfast in bed every morning for six decades. When the Parkinson's made his hands too shaky to carry a tray he brought her tea and toast in a plastic tub. Being a child of a long, painful divorce, I clung to their mythological love story, and the belief that I was destined for one of my own due to my divine origins. Then I became a parent, and discovered how absurdly difficult a relationship could be. Two kids in, Sam and I were officially lost and pretending not to be. If my grandparents' love was a chest of buried treasure, we were trying to find it with a map on the back of a menu at a pirate-themed restaurant.

'Have you guys been up to much lately?' I asked.

'Oh no, we don't do anything these days,' said my grandmother. 'We've got one foot in the grave.'

'Who's we?' said my grandfather. The words were soft and the first he had managed to say since joining the table.

Sam went to coax Dee Dee inside with a sausage roll. Franny stirred in the capsule and I felt the muscles in my breasts contract.

My grandmother told us she had a chicken living in the laundry up until a few days before. She tucked it into a bed of newspaper, with food and water just there, kissed her goodnight and that was that. The old girl drifted away in her sleep, she said.

'Screaming in agony,' added my grandfather.

'Oh, stop it,' she laughed.

'Aaaah aaahhh. Screamed herself to death.'

Sam and I could do with a sprinkle of showmanship. What was the harm in a light shell of make-up, a little lighting, a joke or two? If we could just arm ourselves enough, a shopping list or an eye roll wouldn't have the power to unravel each other's entire coping systems. If we could just find the energy required to build and apply said armour.

Every night, after the kids had gone to bed, we scraped, stacked and sorted like sexless Christmas elves, fell into bed and woke up at two, four and six. We were so deeply in survival mode we had forgotten there was any other way to be. Sometimes we ate dinner, just the two of us, but usually we took our meals standing in the kitchen with Franny and Dee Dee, repeating the words 'tummy' and 'spoon'.

After lunch, Sam took Dee Dee into the patch of rainforest out back, where five years earlier we had said our wedding vows, weak with happiness. My grandmother had put a hand on each of our shoulders and said, 'All our love, I give to you.'

Shouldn't that have been enough?

When describing a movie, meal or walk to the shops, my grandmother leads with the part she loved madly. And there's always something. Beautiful teeth, blackberries on sale, a pot-belly stove at a tense dinner party. She gets to the terrible part eventually—the hokey dialogue and divorce rumours—but doesn't like to dwell. Studies show that an optimistic outlook improves your overall health and longevity, and my grandmother is living proof of the theory. The surgeon who removed her skin cancer last year said she had the arteries of a twenty-year-old, which became the headline of her health update. Even her tumours had a silver lining.

There were happy moments at home, in the madness. Some of the happiest of my life. Like when Sam sang 'Down to the River' with the lights out, wrestling Dee Dee into her pyjamas. She was giggling like a kookaburra mixed with a babbling brook, the sound rushing out of her in a stream. Sam kept the beat like a seasoned professional, working the clothing around her thrashing limbs. Franny, in a rare moment of quiet contemplation, lay on her back with one hand hanging through the bars of her cot, like she was on a boat, running her fingertips along the surface of the water.

My grandmother and I were drinking coffee on the deck. The sun was shining, just, stirring the flowers and birds. She wore a quilted coat printed with a maze of colours. Her eyes were dense blue and watered in the light. She could still see through a bit of one of them.

'Sa-am!' she called to my grandfather in her singsong way, as if it was a joy to say. 'You want coffee?'

'No thanks, Shirl,' he sang back, to the best of his ability.

She kept her marriage fat with love. He appreciated her endlessly.

My Sam returned with Dee Dee on his shoulders. They each wore a flower behind their ear.

'She's crapped,' he said. 'I'll change her.'

'Thanks,' I said. I meant it too.

DR MIMI

I was making snacks to take to Dee Dee's doctor's appointment. We were running late. The television blared, a toddler distraction while I made the snacks and looked for various essentials. I'd found the referral and Medicare card, but no keys.

'Franny, just one cracker. Okay, and one for your sister. No, don't tip them on the ground. Please stop crying. I don't have the patience. Okay, just one more. And one for your sister. We need some for the car and the waiting room and the appointment. It's fine. I'll make more. What time is it? Why can I hear crying in there? No, you're just licking the peanut butter off. You can't have another cracker. Don't hit your sister. Stop crying.'

They both screamed so loudly I felt it in my teeth.

'ENOUGH! ENOUGH! ENOUGH!' I screamed, much louder.

'Mummy, Mummy, Mummy,' Franny said, her arms outstretched, pleading with me to come back.

'Stay here,' I hissed, anger consuming me, a vision of throwing her across the room zigzagging through my head.

I'd crossed over. She could hear it in my voice. I was rage mum. The one who broke things and slammed doors and was hollow inside. Franny fell to the ground like it was crumbling beneath her. Dee Dee was still and quiet, alert, having seen it all before.

I left the room and Franny followed. *Get away from me get away from me get away from me,* I muttered through a clenched jaw, my body covered in spikes. I made it to the bedroom and closed the door with a bang, breathing while she screamed on the other side of it, trying to remember a mantra from the book I'd read on anger management.

'PRESENT MOMENT, WONDERFUL MOMENT!' I screamed, causing Franny to cry even harder.

I opened the door and scooped her into my arms, my rage expressed, making way for tenderness and shame.

We made it to the car and I buckled them into their

seats, giving them snacks and music options. Dee Dee brought the doll she'd been given for her birthday. Dr Mimi accompanied us everywhere, smiling serenely.

'Hiiii,' came a voice over the fence. It was the neighbour I shared a wall with, adopting a pitch at least an octave higher than her usual. She must have heard us.

'Hiiii,' I replied, low and with a nasal undertone, trying my best to politely suggest that she fuck the fuck off.

The sound of her roller door was followed by the crunch of gravel underfoot.

'Hiiii, are you okay?' came her voice from behind the car.

'I don't feel like chatting right now,' I snapped, busying myself with a seatbelt.

'No problem!' she replied in her new octave. 'Have a lovely day!'

I received a text message seconds later.

Neighbour: *Didn't mean to invade your space. Just wanted to give you a hug and check you were ok.*
Me: *No don't be sorry, I appreciate it. Shame spiralling. Thanks for checking in*

We arrived at the doctor's and I checked my phone again.

Neighbour: *Jesus I know that feeling. Don't beat yourself up.*

A - they won't remember
B - they love you regardless
C - you're doing your best

Let me know whenever you just need a break and I can swap in for 10mins or so while you clear your head.

You're not alone.

'Mummy's crying,' said Dee Dee. 'Are you okay mummy?'

'Ohhhh Mummy,' said Franny, her eyes huge with concern.

'I'm okay. I'm sorry for yelling.'

'And then you threw the bowl of rice,' said Dee Dee, struggling to undo her seatbelt.

'That was a while ago, but I'm sorry for that too.' I glanced at the doll on her lap, which blinked twice with Dee Dee's movement.

Seems like she might remember after all, it seemed to imply.

Dr Mimi was a foot tall with a glossy mane that cascaded to the seat of her coral jeans. Her x-rays and stethoscope implied a varied and established medical career, but she didn't take herself too seriously, as demonstrated by her sparkly high-top sneakers. I'd selected her from a range of dolls with special interests, marketed as a way of teaching young girls they could be anything they wanted to be. 'Phoebe' came with a hot pink robot she'd invented, 'Kitty' wore overalls and 'Janet' appeared to be mixed race.

Upon picking her up for the first time, Dr Mimi blinked unexpectedly and Dee Dee threw the doll across the room, unsure whether or not she was dealing with a sentient being. Dee Dee then dropped to the floor and began circling the specimen in a low crawl, feeling her way through the primal version of googling someone.

With her experience in a high-intensity work environment and her painted-on smile, Dr Mimi's patience with small children knew no bounds. She was unflappable in the waiting room, watching unperturbed as Dee Dee littered the carpet with food crumbs and Franny sucked the disease-ridden stuffed animals from the toy box. *That's kids for you*, she seemed to say with the arch of her finely drawn eyebrow. *And besides, it's good for her immune system.*

After the doctor's we went to the park. Cherry blossom trees bloomed along the suburban street. They looked like bouquets, apologies for the grim winter.

Mimi took the swing next to Dee Dee's, her long hair floating behind her as she glided through the air. I pushed them both with Franny on my hip.

'Higher, Mummy! And Mimi too!'

'Ten more then let's try the slide, okay?'

'No, just swing! Mummy no . . . not straight. Make it straight! Good girl, Mummy!'

Mimi's silence was deafening. She knew the consequences of ending a swing session before Dee Dee was ready. She also knew that I was too exhausted to risk a public meltdown. *This is where a little tenacity comes in handy*, said the back of Mimi's head. *You know, when I was working the wards . . .*

And how long ago was that now? I thought, smiling with just my nostrils.

Parents stood in twos and threes around the edges of the park. They traded logistics, gripes and logistical gripes: pick-ups, drop-offs and the need for a pedestrian crossing on this street or that.

'Viva, you need to look after Uma. She was 45 euros, okay?' said a woman in a spotless white shirt. She was holding a stuffed silver unicorn she had rescued from the dirt. She brushed at the smudge for several minutes, long after it had disappeared. The toy's metallic coat shimmered in the sunlight, a beacon of magic and spontaneity, the kind perhaps only available to the woman for purchase.

A toddler ran by holding a soft toy rabbit over her face like a gas mask. When she passed the swings a damp, tangy smell floated after her. I waved to her mother across the playground. We'd met once before. She'd told me of the unfortunate situation regarding her daughter's favourite plaything, aptly named Stinky Bunny.

'I waited too long before getting the backup one,' she had explained. 'It was too clean and new compared to the original. I couldn't fool her. She calls it: Other Bunny.'

'What happens if she doesn't have the stinky one?'

'We went overseas to visit family and it was more important than the passports.'

I gasped.

'It's the only thing that comforts her. Since her dad and I split up, she won't even let me hug her.'

The child sat huffing the mottled animal on a nearby tree stump. She turned it this way and that, every so often removing it from her face and scrunching her nose, having discovered a note so pungent it even gave her pause. But almost immediately she'd return to it, oblivious to her mother's call, disgusted and entranced by her tangle of DNA.

By the gate was a woman wearing a linen jumpsuit in cool grey. The wide-legged pant spoke to her modesty and pragmatism, while the cloth belt around her waist suggested a nod to maintaining one's femininity during a demonstration of brute emotional and physical strength. Her toddler was clinging to her leg screeching like a demon that had clambered out of another realm. The mother's hands were linked at the back of her head and her face was tilted upwards towards the sun, chest open, summoning the strength of God herself. She remained like that for a minute or so while the child continued to cry. Had I surveyed the other park-goers, they might have described the duration of time as 'uncomfortable'. Eventually the woman manoeuvred her child, thrashing, into the little seat attached to her bicycle and arched her neck to secure her helmet under her chin. The child continued their protest as she rode slowly away, the screams growing softer, but not to her.

Mimi gazed approvingly from the high end of the seesaw. *Now that's how you keep your act together,* she blinked.

$10 bucks says she rides into the lake, I replied under my breath, helping Dee Dee off and letting Mimi hit the tanbark with a thud.

'Do you remember sad things about me or happy things?' I asked Dee Dee in the car. It was a year or so later. We were on our way to meet Georgie.

'Um,' she looked down at her legs. 'Sad things.'

My rage was less frequent, and rarely inspired a

check-in from the neighbour, Fiona, my friend by that stage.

'That's okay to remember sad things,' I smiled reassuringly, feeling as though I might be sick. 'What about Daddy?'

'Happpppyyyyyyyyyyyy!' she said, grinning and throwing her arms in the air.

I told Georgie at the play centre and dropped my head into my hands.

'You can't say this to me,' she said. 'I'm too pregnant.' She heaved herself from her chair and kneeled on the floor in front of me, placing her hands firmly on my shoulders. 'She loves you so much, Ashe. You're doing a great job.'

Georgie returned to her chair and blew her nose on a napkin. It was unusual to see her cry. Ordinarily she preferred to sweat her tears out at the gym. Overall, she was still the same person she had always been. It was soothing to be around. Growing up, I had a Cabbage Patch doll named Sally that I adored, but who only offered a fraction of the comfort I got from my big sister. Despite my pleas, Georgie refused to let me sleep in her bed, but would tolerate me sleeping next to it. I'd take my pillow and blanket and set up camp in a wooden wagon I'd have dragged alongside her, my legs spilling over the edge and hand tucked discreetly under her doona.

To our left, Dee Dee and her cousin stood frozen in terror at the top of an inflatable slide.

'I'll get them down,' I said, rice cake crumbs falling from my lap onto the floor.

'Nah, they're being pussies,' said Georgie.

She pushed her chair back and walked over to the bottom of the slide.

'You scared?' she asked through a veil of inquisitiveness. 'Aww, you're scared,' she said again, this time dropping the question mark altogether.

Evidently, Georgie's two-year-old was no pussy. Estele narrowed her eyes and launched herself head-first down the slide, into her mother's chiselled arms. Dee Dee succumbed to the pressure and followed shortly after. Franny ran to join us and the five of us jumped up and down on the mat, victorious.

'Do you want to do crafts before we go?' I asked.

'It's okay,' said Dee Dee. 'I did farts already.'

Dr Mimi was unremarkably absent. Over time, her friend status had been reduced from permanent fixture to occasional tea party guest. The months of having a toddler as her primary carer had ravaged her. She looked less like a fun-loving doctor and more like she was between houses, having lost all her possessions in a fire. Her once-shiny mane was matted and dull, her instruments of medicine long gone. One high-top remained, but it had warped in the sun, leaving her feet scuffed and bare. Every so often, I'd comb her hair into a ponytail and sponge the texta from her face. Sometimes after the kids had gone to bed, I'd mix her a thimble of gin and tonic and prop her onto the deck chair next to mine, exhaling after the long day. Hard times had made her tolerable.

THE SLUG: PART I

Twenty years on I can still feel it pop. My right foot tingles at the memory, just beneath my second and third toe, tattooed on my sole. It was night. The bathroom of my family home was dark apart from an intrusion of moonlight through the window shutters. The slug was in the shadows, its wet body across the path of my naked foot. I'll remember the sound always, no louder than the burst of a bubble, a gentle thunk, as if it was made of air.

It wasn't made of air.

There's nothing more loathsome than a slug. They are thumbs of mucus writhing in slow motion, relentless on their path of destruction yet completely unarmed, fearless despite their raw, dribbling fragility. *Shells are for the weak*, I imagine them hissing through tens of thousands of soft microscopic teeth.

My mother was the first to arrive at the scene, and was enraged to discover the cause of my distress.

'For fuck's sake, Ashe! I thought you were being murdered!'

'Well I'm sorry to disappoint you, MUM. ERGHHHH, the slime! It's EVERYWHERE!'

'Just wipe it with some toilet paper and go back to bed. You're going to wake up the entire street.'

'ARE YOU CRAZY? I CAN'T TOUCH IT! NO! NO! NOOOOOOOO!'

'Jesus goddamn Christ. Then move yourself. Now. NOW.'

I could hear her retching in the bathroom as she disposed of the remains. I was in the laundry filling the sink with scalding water for a medical-grade foot bath.

With a final flush my mother turned off the light and stomped back to her room, collapsing on her bed with an exasperated groan. I held up my middle finger at the darkened alcove between the laundry and the bathroom, using my free hand to pour in a cap of Pine O Cleen.

I turned off the tap, and the water enveloped my feet in a sterile embrace.

I was in year ten and on the verge of being expelled from school. Between ages thirteen and fourteen I'd gone from a musical-loving, braces-wearing wing attack to a smoking, swearing hellcat. I attended mandatory appointments with the school counsellor for my attitude problem. Prior to her, there had been a string of Family Court–appointed psychologists, hired to deliver insights that could be used on either side of my parents' decade-long case. Puppets were a popular child psychology device in the nineties, but few embodied the particular charisma required for a successful puppetry performance. I recall a lot of sock puppet work. Just something from the drawer at home, fashioned with googly eyes and a squeaky voice devoid of character development. I acted out at school, stealing from the canteen, smoking at Sovereign Hill and pushing Vanessa on the netball court, but the final nail in my expulsion was telling a teacher to get fucked.

'This isn't the place for you,' the principal said later in his office, sitting in the chair next to mine. 'Go and clean out your locker. Your mother's on her way.'

My bad behaviour continued long after high school. I got fired from hospitality jobs for being rude to customers. At home I yelled and broke things. I road-raged and betrayed best friends and boyfriends. During my twenties, I saw a psychoanalyst who worked above an abortion clinic, where I'd pretend I was getting a weekly abortion to the pro-lifers who picketed the entrance.

'Whoopsie!' I giggled when I passed them the first time.

'I've been a bad, bad baby,' I whispered the following week to an old man who was brandishing a mangled doll.

'What do you think is the cause of your anger?' the psychoanalyst asked.

'Anger,' I said. 'Anger is the cause of my anger.'

'Mmmmmmmmmmm.' She gave a gooey fretful smile. 'I understand it might feel that way. But we tend to think of anger more as a symptom of something else, something deeper.'

She gestured to a poster on the wall designed to explain anger to children. In the middle was a red-faced cartoon cat with steam coming out of its ears. Lines shot outwards towards illustrations of the deeper emotions of which she spoke, things like hurt, shame, sadness and fear. It was as if she'd opened the door to a murky, underground cellar, reeking of mould and damp.

I spoke about some of the more stressful parts of my childhood, which the therapist believed to be 'imperative to my healing'. Afterwards I called in sick to work and sat shivering on a bench by the river.

'I don't care what's causing it,' I said during my third and final session. 'I just want to be able to control it.'

'Some wounds need more than a bandaid,' she said.

'Yeah, a bandaid's good for now, thanks.'

She gave me the name of a cognitive behavioural therapist who I never called and things stayed much the same.

Shortly after Dee Dee was born, Sam and I moved to a house in the suburbs. When the last of the furniture had been packed into the truck, a curation of my rage remained on display in the empty rooms. Chipped tiles from saucepans I'd hurled across the kitchen, cracked doors and red wine stains that trailed along the textured walls.

A small part of me hoped becoming a mother would endow me with the serenity of a sea cow and a wardrobe of flowing organic linen, but in reality, it gave me more to be furious about than ever before, and practically obliterated my desire for nice clothes. I slammed nursery doors and screamed gutturally in the car. Once stuck in traffic with Dee Dee crying, I clenched my jaw so hard I cracked my tooth. Typically, after a rage episode, I'd sink into a period of depression, which would eventually fuel my anger, and so on.

I stopped seeing anyone, citing work and child-rearing as the justification for my near complete isolation. My sister Parris went away and left me the key to her apartment, the idea being that I would get a few good nights' sleep and everything would be okay.

The place was spotless and the sheets were clean. Perfectly maintained plants swung gently in baskets that hung from the ceiling. It was three stories up and featured a balcony I couldn't go anywhere near, the thought of jumping like a burst of fresh air.

Slugs have male and female genitalia, which means they can self-fertilise to produce offspring. I was self-fertilising suffering only to breed more suffering, but I had only the faintest idea of the scale of it. Following me everywhere was a terrestrial slug of hatred, the size of three minivans at least. I imagine it had been tailing me for the majority of my adult life, swathed in a wet armless trench coat, a pair of sunglasses perched atop its long tentacles. It's a wonder I didn't discover it sooner.

THE LAST THING I WILL SEE BEFORE I DIE

When my sister Parris and Sam's brother Toby started dating, a dream I never knew I had came true. After my initial concerns over whether or not it was incest were put to rest, I moved quickly to a deep appreciation of their union. Finally, I had someone to engage in base conversation with at Sam's notoriously sophisticated family affairs.

'What do you mean you don't watch porn?' Parris demanded at one such occasion.

'I tried one of those sites for women and watched someone go to town on herself in a marble bathroom,' I whispered. 'There was a disturbing volume of fluid.'

'Oh.' Parris took a delicate sip of her wine. 'It's always piss.'

'Also, she was naked apart from a pair of flesh-toned kitten heels.'

'Haunting,' said Parris.

'What are you two cackling about?' asked Sam's father, topping up our glasses.

'Film,' we said in unison.

We were a regular Snow White and Rose Red. We had found our matching princes in the magical forest and were now free to ignore them completely and talk about female ejaculation. I basked in having someone I could let it all hang out with at my in-laws'. Plus, Parris and Toby were child-free, with no plans to start a family in the immediate future. This was a perk on two counts: not only did they have a vested interest in our kids, they each had a free pair of hands to help with them. Their children, if or when they had them, would be double cousins with ours, which was positively royal. Family get-togethers would become a real-life face swap, as our gene pools congealed into one miscellaneous spread. The next 40 years clicked lazily into place. There was just one problem. Parris looked kind of like me and Toby looked kind of like Sam, and they were each several years younger than us, which meant that at least once a week we came face to face with the fresher, more in love, pre-children versions of ourselves.

In the six months since Franny had arrived, Sam and I had been on two dates. The first was a rushed bowl of pho before a couples counselling session and the second was a rushed bowl of pho after a couples counselling session. Parris and Toby's dating life, on the other hand, was flashy and elaborate, as if it had been designed by the production department of *The Bachelor.*

'You look tanned—where have you been?' I asked Parris in my laundry one afternoon.

'Didn't I tell you? We went horse-riding through the Snowy Mountains.'

'What do you mean?'

'Toby surprised me for my birthday.' Her expression shifted to accommodate a wave of guilt and pity. 'Pretty over the top, right?'

'Wait, what have you been doing?' I was sorting through a pile of ant-infested clothes with Franny on my hip.

'You know, like, riding horses through mountains . . . in New South Wales.'

'You're not making any sense,' I said, almost shouted.

She laughed then became serious, her years of nursing equipping her with a keen sense for the early signs of a neurological event. 'Are you okay?'

'Cannot compute, cannot compute,' I said in a robot voice, jealousy momentarily taking hold of my body and soul. 'I'm kidding. I'm okay. Where did you sleep?'

'In a tent.' She held out a photo on her phone. 'It rained overnight, which was overkill. I asked Toby to pull back on the romance after that.'

'Of course it did,' I muttered, zooming in on the picnic rug spread out by the tent, where a wheel of brie was savouring its last spectacular view.

I'd suggested couples counselling for the same reason anybody does: to have an objective third party confirm that I was right about everything and he was the problem. Don't get me wrong, I'm the first to admit my flaws. I just share them in carefully measured doses so as to appear vulnerable as a way of controlling a situation. Our counsellor observed that about me during our second session and recommended I seek out my own private therapy as well.

Inspired by his younger brother's grand, romantic gestures, Sam surprised me by booking a weekend away for us and the girls.

'It's a bit out of our price range,' he said, beaming, 'but I think we deserve it.'

I scrolled through photos of a lofty beach house. 'And the check-in's on a Friday? Don't you have to work?'

'I've taken the afternoon off.'

'Great, which means I'll be getting the kids organised and packing the car and you get to swoop in with the keys to the glamorous house. That's just perfect.'

'I can pack the car the night before,' he said, deflated.

'Hey, Mum,' said Dee Dee. 'Hey, Dad.'

'I appreciate you doing this,' I seethed, 'but I would have rather planned it together.'

'Talk to me,' said Dee Dee, who was sitting at the kitchen bench.

'Yes, Dee Dee?' said Sam.

Her eyes darted around for a new topic. 'Das a big, big punkin.'

'It is a big pumpkin,' I said. 'Even bigger than your head!'

'Don't be angwee at my daddy anymore.'

I nodded. 'Okay.'

The pumpkin soup would be our last family meal for some time. While eating it, Dee Dee had been harbouring a strain of gastro that would rip through our family and colour our bed linen orange for the next four days. Weak with dehydration, we would murmur encouraging sentiments to each other about the approaching getaway, which quickly took on mythical healing properties in our minds. We scrolled tenderly through the photos of the property listing, with its wraparound balcony and ocean views, promising an unfathomable amount of fresh air and light. After four days and four nights of trudging from the bedroom to the bathroom to the laundry of our small cluttered home, the day arrived when we would journey to the Promised Land.

Not long after we pulled out of the driveway both the girls fell asleep. I looked over my shoulder and breathed them in.

'Dee Dee's hair looks so good,' I said.

'I know,' said Sam. 'Are they a boy or a girl? No, they're better. Like David Bowie.'

Dee Dee had never looked smaller than in the barber's chair for her buzz cut a few days earlier. It was my latest attempt to deter her from pulling out her hair. She sat on a booster seat in a lime green gown that brushed the floor. Every few seconds she would turn her head to check I was still there, not fully trusting the reflection.

The girls slept most of the drive and the freeway shimmered with hope. That's the thing about gastro: when it finally passes things have never looked or smelled so good. I mentioned this to Sam and he agreed, likening the feeling to finding a soft bed in a jungle of thorns. Parris and Toby were set to join us for the second night of our holiday, which I was looking forward to. I wanted to take Sam out for dinner that night to plan adventures, like we used to.

For the last ten minutes of the trip, we drove slowly through a labyrinth of gravel streets named Foam and Spray while both girls screamed and screamed.

'I can't, I can't, I can't,' I was saying under my breath, my legs curled up on the passenger seat.

'We're here,' said Sam.

Between the white couches, clusters of delicate trinkets displayed at knee-height and collection of documentaries on DVD, the house was clear on its stance on children: Bring them if you must, but please leave their batteries at home. There was no Snakes and Ladders or Connect Four in the collection of board games. Games were not a childish pastime, according to the property owner. They were a battle of wits, to be played by a gathering of adults looking to spar over Scrabble and a bottle of shiraz, when things got wild and loose after the viewing of a documentary on birds. At least they had Monopoly.

I stepped onto the balcony to take in the ocean view, but could only see as far as the cable railing, which featured toddler-sized gaps and a four-metre drop to the ground. It was early evening and the winter light was rapidly disappearing. Inside came the sound of 5000 jigsaw pieces raining softly onto kitchen tiles.

'What toys do we have?' asked Sam, his head appearing through the sliding door.

'Beats me,' I said, my eyes trained on the view. 'Which ones did you pack?'

Sam made dinner while I breastfed Franny and Dee Dee put the Monopoly thimble in her mouth without us seeing.

'Ashe! Ashe!' Sam said, in a voice I hadn't heard before.

I ran to them. Dee Dee was coughing and crying. Sam was holding the thimble.

'It was stuck in her throat,' he said. 'I felt it with my finger.'

'Oh my God, oh my God.'

'I hit her on the back and it came out.'

Our therapist had encouraged us to sit quietly together as a way to reset. Some part of us had to be touching, an arm or hand or a leg. Touching was homework these days. We tried it after the kids had gone to bed, but it quickly turned into a verbal assignment. He shared with me that he was still reeling over the choking incident and needing comfort. I shared with him that he needed to get a grip. I was reeling too. I needed comfort. But when I reached out I was met with panicking arms. Two people drown faster than one. All the more limbs to flail. All the more downward momentum.

The next morning, I was lying on a makeshift single bed in the study when I heard a car pull into the driveway. Moments later, the fresher, happier, more attractive, well rested, more in love versions of Sam and me ascended the polished staircase. They came bearing outdoor activity equipment and things to make s'mores.

There are no s'mores here, I wanted to hiss through a crack in the door, like the Ghost of Relationship

Yet to Come, *only separate bedrooms and the omnipresence of death.*

Parris wore tailored pants, a soft knitted turtleneck and brogues that had only recently emerged from a shoebox. Her blonde hair was swept into a ponytail, allowing an unobstructed view of her sparkling eyes and nourished skin.

'Holy crap, you look amazing,' I said, emerging from the study with a screech of the sliding door.

'Thank you!' she said, in the exaggerated way we do.

'That outfit looks like it cost a thousand dollars.'

'I mean, more if you count the sunglasses,' she said.

We laughed with the expensively dressed scamp. The air felt lighter.

Toby and Dee Dee were deep in conversation. Something about a 'cockadoo'. Parris and he had recently stayed at a house in the rainforest. On the first night they played strip backgammon and ate wheels of cheese. It was a clash of activities, Parris explained, leaving it there. Their second mistake was planning too many activities over the following few days. Between the day spas and hikes and waterfall photo ops, they didn't get to 'enjoy' the accommodation as much as they would have liked.

'You didn't get to sit in as many chairs as you wanted?' asked Sam. 'What does that mean?'

'Yeah,' I snorted, resisting the urge to aggressively high-five him. 'Like a cat?'

Sam and I laughed loudly, united in bitterness.

I feigned enthusiasm when a trip to the beach was suggested.

'Should we drive?' I asked. 'How far is it?'

'It's only a ten-minute walk,' said Sam, putting on his hat. The breezy holiday guy.

'So a schlep with a baby and a toddler,' I smiled.

At home, I conducted the kids' dinner and bath procession with a slowing tempo, the light outside fading and our voices becoming soft. Sam would get home and chase them down the hallway and around their bedroom, so they laughed hysterically until one of them cried and clung to me, wired and fluttering. I'd scrape the hardened food off the floor while he read them stories. The fun guy. The happy things guy.

Parris and Toby's arrival had confirmed that four was the civilised number of parents required per family. The time it normally took to leave the house was neatly cut in half. Toby located the missing toddler shoe and Parris took out the rubbish and returned with the sunscreen from the glove box of our car. Together, they carried the esky along the gravel road leading to the beach. I wore Franny in the carrier and Sam had Dee Dee on his shoulders. Tea-trees twisted either side of the path, splintered from the salty air.

Sam talked about the food he planned to prepare for dinner; seafood and complicated salads and spicy dips. I hadn't told him about my plan to whisk him away on a date night and winced over the fact that he hadn't thought to ask me. I hadn't gone so far as to book anything or mention it to anyone. Nor did I particularly feel up for the pressure to Reconnect, but I slowed my pace anyway so that I was several metres behind the group, burdened with the full responsibility of keeping the romance alive.

Cockatoos screeched and galahs squabbled in the treetops. The ocean grew loud and wild. The path from the road to the beach was steep and narrow. Franny swivelled her head in alarm. She'd never been to the beach. I held the railing so as not to lose my balance, already annoyed about having to walk back up, conscious of making it in time for Franny's nap. Sam was looking up at us from the sand with a peculiar look on his face. Dee Dee was still on his shoulders, tugging desperately at her clothes. She was afraid of a lot of things: spiders, *Boss Baby*, an imaginary hippo in the toy box and Yannis, the overzealous carer from daycare. The Pacific Ocean, on the other hand, didn't faze her. She craned towards it, her shaved head no longer a symbol of anxiety, but rather, the preferred hairstyle of any sea huntress worth their salt. Once they reached the sand she ran towards the water wearing nothing at all, Sam and Toby at her heels.

Franny clung to me with every working muscle in her body when I tried to put her on the sand. Eventually she settled on Parris's lap, from where she peered sceptically at her surrounds.

'We're not in a good place,' I said, rummaging through the nappy bag.

'Oh no, what's happening?' she asked.

'I'm just angry at him. All the time.'

'You're probably just tired and over it.'

I looked at her unlined, hopeful face. Her forehead not yet concave.

'That's true, but he leaves dirty nappies in the hallway and it makes me want to harm him.'

'Uh-ohh,' she said in a singsong baby voice, wiggling Franny's miniature toes.

'Motherhood's a scam. I wish I'd known how much harder life would be, and how I'd have so little energy to deal with it all, and how a dirty nappy in the hall could make me feel worthless, you know? Maybe I wouldn't be so angry.'

'But maybe then you wouldn't have done it.'

I watched Franny gasp the salty air with a licking motion, like it was a new and scintillating dish.

'Yeah, that's a scary thought.'

Parris and Toby showered together when we

returned from the beach. Laughter bounced from the bathroom into the stairwell. Sam made dinner and I kept the children from falling through the balcony railing. I wanted to knock loudly on their door like a teacher at camp. *Break it up, you two. You wouldn't eat a Sunday roast in front of starving people, would you? Have some consideration.*

We ate outside while the sun was setting, like a photo from an Airbnb listing. Throughout the meal, a neighbouring Rottweiler barked like it wanted to kill us all. Next to it, a woman kneeled and tended to her garden, unconcerned, either out of passive hostility or total deafness. Parris was quiet and Toby asked her if she was okay. She said she was, and later confessed to me that she was suffering from terrible gas. That's why she kept making up reasons to go inside, so she could relieve herself away from her attentive new boyfriend. It made me feel better. I thanked her for telling me.

In bed, Sam told me how capable I'd looked on the narrow steps against the wildness of the beach and the wind. He said it might be the last thing he saw before he died. I told him I had a similar feeling looking down at him, now that he mentioned it. Though I hadn't put it into words in my mind. His sturdy shoulders under Dee Dee's frantic enthusiasm. Their similarities and absurd height difference. The dark blue ocean crashing and foaming behind them.

Maybe I just wanted to say something romantic back. I knew the feeling, though. I experienced it often. We fell asleep holding hands.

A few hours later, I awoke to Sam calling out from the bathroom. The light was on. I stumbled out of bed towards it.

'I'm cramping really badly,' he said, from the toilet.

'You ate too much of that garlic dip at dinner,' I said, annoyed.

The dip was so pungent that Toby and Parris had avoided it completely, a wordless agreement that it was too soon in the relationship.

'Can you please stay here?' he asked. His worried eyebrows gave his face more of an oval shape than usual. He looked like a cartoon of a concerned person. I almost laughed.

'I think I'm about to faint,' he said. 'I'm scared I'm going to hit my head.'

'It's okay. I'm here. We're going to get through this.' I was awake then, my mind clear.

He grimaced as another cramp rolled through his body and I readied myself to support his head should he fall, neither of us breaking eye contact. A voluminous bowel evacuation soon followed. A bucketful, at least.

'I'm okay,' he said, his eyebrows returned to their resting position, his face a regular shape again.

'Okay.' I stumbled back to bed.

Neither of us mentioned it in the morning. Disgustingly intimate moments happened often enough in our relationship. We surrendered ourselves totally to one another's support on a daily basis. It was part of the job description since becoming parents. There was something about the light in the bathroom, though. The way it cut through the open sliding door. His face searching desperately for mine, the two of us banded together for as long as it goes. The pungency of the smell to really seal the memory. In all likelihood, it will be the last thing I see before I die.

'ME TIME' IN COOBER PEDY

I used to enjoy socialising with people. At least I think I did. A standard Saturday night would involve drinking two bottles of wine, so it's possible I used to enjoy socialising with hat stands. These days, my idea of a good time is eating an Easter egg alone in my car. It happened recently and the experience left me with a feeling of tranquillity akin to a Japanese bathhouse session on a rainy weekday.

I'd just bought the second-cheapest set of sheets from Homewares Galore, and had decided to treat myself with a choccy goog from the display at the checkout. It was a Friday night, after all. Sam was home with the kids and I was free to ring in the weekend any way my heart desired, which was by purchasing sheets and going to sleep, obviously—just as soon as I got me some egg. I carefully peeled back the gleaming purple tinfoil, the delicate metallic scrunch the only sound inside the otherwise tomb-like car. I rolled the chocolate around my mouth slowly, transfixed by an abandoned trolley edging across the car park towards a Mercedes-Benz with the number plate RUNVS 7.

On the way home I drove past my neighbour, a mother of three, sitting at a pottery wheel in her garage. She was dressed in a pair of clay-splattered overalls and a red bandana, which I suspected was more for mood-enhancing purposes rather than function given that she had a pixie cut. In that moment, Kerry wasn't a full-time HR manager and 24-hour mum but, rather, an artist at work in her studio. The people mover wedged in beside her and the greenish overhead lighting did nothing to dispel the fantasy. She was lost in the clay, eyes closed, mere moments away from summoning the ghost of Patrick Swayze himself.

'Me time' is a thing parents are meant to embrace to stave away insanity. It might involve reading a book, catching up with a friend or drinking a cup of tea in the bedroom with the door closed. People without children might refer to it simply as 'time'. The idea is to carve out a moment in the day to call your own, a healthy reminder that you are a person *as well as* a faceless organism that's been biologically programmed to nourish its young. It's the reason you will often find me in our back shed at the end of a particularly long day. What it lacks in warmth it makes up for with a sense of stillness, save for the occasional passing rodent, and a door with a lock. I'll dust off a sleeping bag, curl up on a camping chair and watch clips from *The Golden Girls* until I fall asleep—jolting awake to a possum thundering across the tin roof.

It was during one of these shed sessions that I got a call from my dear friend Abi.

'Hey, what are you doing?' she asked.

'Just, ah …' I tried to think of something that wouldn't sound too tragic to a child-free person with a job in the arts. *Think brain, think. You're a person, remember? Just say you're doing something person-y.* 'I'm making frittata!'

'Yum. So, I'm heading to the outback this weekend for work and I've got a spare plane ticket. Wanna come?'

'No' had become my standard response to most things. No, I couldn't come to the outback. Was she insane? Why would she even ask? I was drifting through a cloud of sleep deprivation and an unchecked case of postnatal depression. My comfort zone lay within a 200-metre radius of my house. It had a park, library, cafe with a toy box, supermarket and an Italian restaurant on the corner for the date night we fully intended to book a babysitter for. The thought of flying interstate with a single carry-on bag was absurd. What was I going to do? Sleep? At night? By myself? Then what? Wake up when I felt like it? When it was light outside? It was preposterous. Terrifying. Obscene.

There was a rustle under the ski jacket in the corner of the darkened shed. A possum maybe, or a family of rats.

'Yesh,' I said suddenly, the unfamiliar word sluggish on my tongue. 'Yes! I'd love to come.'

A few days later, Abi and I were in a cab on our way to the airport. It was 5 a.m., but naturally the children picked the morning of my departure to sleep in. I snuck in and kissed their hot sleeping faces goodbye.

'Mummy go to work,' Dee Dee mumbled.

'Back to sleep, honey.'

'I back asweep now.' She resumed snoring like a pug.

We were heading to a remote opal mining town called Coober Pedy. It has a population of around 2500, most of whom live in underground houses called 'dugouts'. They were a people who valued personal space so much they carved it out with picks and shovels. I couldn't wait to not meet them.

Childless, the domestic departures terminal was my

own non-sexual pleasure palace. I finished not one but two coffees before they went cold, and read an entire magazine undisturbed. It felt naughty and delicious, like calling in sick to work from a blow-up flamingo in your friend's pool. My meals at home were generally made up of whatever remained on the kids' plates, which I ate crouched by the bin in my dressing-gown, eyes darting, ready to throw my body in front of a permanent marker that was about to make contact with a wall.

The breakfast options in the food court stretched out in front of me like a neon-lit Roman banquet. My eyes feasted on the overpriced toasties and various deep-fried goo, everything served in darling individual boxes that could be mine and mine alone. I ordered an egg-and-bacon roll with the hottest chilli sauce they had. With my mouth on fire and nose dripping like a tap, I cackled quietly into my sandwich in a booth across from Abi, who would occasionally peer over her book and softly shake her head.

The flight to Adelaide was short, but the drive from there to Coober Pedy was nine long hours. The Stuart Highway is an interminable straight road through a sweltering orange dust pit with not a single piece of Lego as far as the eye can see. It was spectacular. With no phone reception, entertainment was limited to non-baby-related conversation (during which I contributed some thoughts on picture messaging, Y2K and the late great Whitney Houston). Music was limited to the only album I had saved on my phone: *Secrets* by Toni Braxton. We aimed to arrive before dark, as driving at night in the outback was a fairly sure way to die due to oncoming trucks and various wildlife. The wiry clerk at the only servo for 300 kilometres reiterated the dangers to us in fluent Strayan.

'You sheilas wanna get there well before last light or you'll do yerselves a mischief. No fartin' around, got it? Road trains go like cut cats along 'ere and the suicidal roos come out at dusk.'

By the 150th rendition of 'Unbreak My Heart' the light was beginning to fade. We pulled off at a rest stop to spend the night. The sign was accurate. It was a place to rest and stop. And that concluded the list of available amenities. There were no toilets, showers, food, water or lights. It was simply a patch of dirt by the side of the highway hundreds of kilometres from civilisation. It would have been bath time at home. I thought about the girls wrapped in towels and missed them so much I almost started hyperventilating.

Soon stars covered the sky like liquid glitter. We ate muesli bars and talked about our families. Abi's mother died when we were in our twenties. Julia had big hair and a bigger presence, like a perpetual burst of lime and passionfruit. The space she left was as vast and silent as the surrounding desert. I reclined my seat and curled towards my friend, away from the darkness outside. Eventually, stillness came, even peace. I slept for seven dreamless hours.

A mob of kangaroos stood motionless around the car in the morning. Behind them was a carpet of earth and shrub that stretched towards an oozing orange sunrise.

'I have to pee,' Abi whispered, 'but I don't want to get kicked up the arse by one of these roos.'

I said I thought I would hold mine.

Abi started the car and they bounded away. With the engine running, we got out and relieved ourselves. I watched the roos disappear into the untamed country and felt something flicker from within, a part of myself that had long been dormant. I turned to face the rising sun.

We got to Coober Pedy around 9 a.m. It had taken a cab, a plane ride, a nine-hour drive and a sleepover in the desert, but we had finally made it to the edge of the earth. Coober Pedy looked like the place you drank your last pint and took your last piss before tumbling into the void.

Abi had chosen an underground hotel for us to stay in, a popular architectural choice in the area due to the blistering heat. At the front desk was a yellow-bearded man named Martin. After prying a couple of towels from a hardened pile, he growled, 'This way, ladies,' and limped down the underground warren that led to our room.

Ours was the last room at the end of a long dimly lit corridor of sandstone cells.

'I love what you've done with the place, Martin,' I said, widening my eyes in Abi's direction. 'Very *Kiss the Girls*.'

'What's that, a movie, eh?'

'Yeah, with Ashley Judd.'

'Never heard of 'im. Here we are, girls. Make yerselves at home. Sing out if you need anything.'

The small space was dwarfed further by an enormous wooden bunk bed.

'Do you mind taking the top bunk?' asked Abi. 'I get a bit claustrophobic.'

'Sure.' I climbed the ladder to take a closer look. 'Wow, it's pretty close to the ceiling.'

'Yeah, looks like a strictly-for-sleeping kind of set-up. Is it okay?'

I dusted some pink sandstone particles off the rough grey blanket.

'It's perfect,' I coughed.

We settled in and went to explore the town. It was almost ten o'clock. Ordinarily, I'd have already prepared several tiny meals by now, played the same number of intricate mind games in an attempt to get them eaten, and taken a stick and blowtorch to the remnants that had dried like cement to the floor. The shops were closed under a stark blue sky. Abi took some photos of a spaceship wedged in the sandstone across the street, a prop from an old sci-fi movie filmed there. We walked to the sound of her camera lens and our boots on the gravel until we reached the edge of the township.

I inspected my near-empty water bottle. 'I need to sit down.'

'What about this place?' said Abi.

She pointed her camera at a little sign that read *Crazy Bob's B&B.* The front yard of the property was littered with structures made from scrap metal and other debris—a ten-foot robot composed of rusted corrugated iron, a beer bottle pyramid, a giant tin pelican with googly eyes and several great lumps of cast iron painted to look like magic mushrooms. A man appeared at the top of the driveway and waved enthusiastically. He was slight of build, but fast, like one of those desert lizards that really zip across the sand.

'You ladies looking for a place to stay?' he asked.

'Oh—no, thank you,' I replied.

'We were just admiring your sculptures,' said Abi.

'Ah! Yes. This is my art. I make it in my spare time. My name's Bob.' He held out his hand.

'As in the Bob? Crazy Bob?'

'That's what they call me!'

'Pleasure to meet you, Bob. Why do they call you crazy?'

'Because of my art!'

'It's wonderful!' said Abi. 'Mind if I take some photos?'

We followed him up the long dusty driveway until we reached the kitchen—which was outdoor and consisted of a wood-burning stove, a shade cloth and a raised veggie patch. The bed was singular, in a small dugout a few meters from the kitchen. As far as breakfast went, Bob's guests could expect a spoonful of oats and whatever happened to be growing in the patch that day. Bob offered us a habanero chilli that had recently sprouted.

'I just plant the seeds of whatever I eat,' he explained. 'Something always pops up eventually.'

'Do you go to the supermarket in town?' I asked.

'I try not to go to town if I can avoid it. Much too busy for me.'

Bob spent his days mining for opal and repurposing the other stuff he found. He'd been in love once, a long time ago. When it fell apart, he came to Coober Pedy to find his fortune and stayed because he didn't know what else to do.

'The hustle and bustle is getting too much for me,'

he said, gesturing towards the ghostly, barren land that surrounded his home. 'But I won't be here for much longer. I have a dugout two hundred and fifty k's north. I'm going to retire there to search for gold.'

'I hope you find it,' said Abi.

'Thank you, kind lady. Now, let me show you everything that's available for purchase.'

A sales-heavy departure ensued. I bought a family of bottle-cap dolls. Abi selected a tin swan and a rock painted to look like a hamburger.

Back in town, we ordered cheese and Vegemite rolls from the bakery. It was midday and a few miners were taking their lunch break. They moved in single file towards the cash register and placed their orders without making eye contact.

'G'day, Timmo,' said the shopkeeper. 'I haven't seen you in a year! Where ya been?'

'Just work, I s'pose,' said Timmo, his cheeks reddening. I wanted to hug him. 'Pig-dog, thanks, Lorraine.'

'No worries, darlin'.'

A pig-dog was a Coober Pedy special, the brutal cousin of a pig in a blanket. They were a popular choice. Lorraine knew her customers, and their preference for eating somewhere other than her bakery. Abi and I sat on the only two chairs, grubby white and plastic, just inside the door. The window was cracked at boot height. It looked like it had happened the night before. We had heard the town could be a different place after dark, when alcohol was involved. Lorraine was chipper considering the damage to her shop front, though I had no reference for her general mood.

Later at the hotel we played pool with Martin. He was friendlier than when we'd met. He wasn't a morning person, he explained. He was also a week shy of leaving the job, with plans to go travelling with the love of his life.

'I didn't have you pegged as a romantic, Martin,' I said. 'Who's the better half?'

'She's right there.' He jerked his cigarette in the direction of the mini bus parked out the front.

'What are you lovebirds going to do?' asked Abi.

'Go west,' he said dreamily.

'Good for you, Martin,' I said, gazing east, longing for home.

THE RAT

Growing up, we had a black cat called Oscar who moonlighted as a serial killer. His victims were mostly mice and rats, but occasionally he would murder a rosella or galah or some equally vibrant local bird. We always treated the bird cases as the most tragic. My sisters and I would walk slower that day, our voices lowered. Parris might have worn a feather in her hair to honour the fallen. To my mother, it didn't matter what species lay slain on the doormat; all were created equally unbearable. She refused to remove them and my sisters and I followed suit.

Oscar's victims would remain untouched for several days. That entrance to our home would simply be cancelled until further notice. My mother would place two strips of masking tape in a giant X on either side of the door. Sometimes the front and back doors would be off limits and the laundry window was the only access point to the house. Eventually, a neighbour's teenage son would stumble up our driveway with a shovel, and leave with the memory of a clothesline of bras and underwear fluttering in the breeze.

Avoidance was a tactic my mother reserved solely for dead or dying animals. She once put our goldfish tank down the side of the house because she found the fish bobbing at the bottom of the tank. She assumed they were about to die and couldn't bring herself to flush them. Weeks passed before the tank was discovered by one of my sisters. To everybody's horror, the fish were not only alive, but twice the size, having grown strong feeding on the sludge that had gathered in their blackened, unfiltered tank.

Generally speaking, my mother didn't flinch easily. In almost every other aspect of her life she confronted things head on. When I was fourteen, I snuck out to a backyard house party and she appeared at my shoulder in her dressing-gown like the terry-clothed Grim Reaper.

'Home time,' she said simply, then dragged me through the crowd of terror-struck year eights and hurled me into the back of the Tarago.

My father was similarly avoidant when it came to dead rodents, but his strategy was to train us as his own personal crime scene cleaners. He called it a 'bravery contest', and at the snap of a mouse trap the siren would sound. The prize might have been a packet of Tiny Teddies or a half-consumed roll of Quick-Eze he found in his jacket, but the physical reward was irrelevant. We saw our father every second weekend, which made his approval alone a big ticket item. It was covetable enough to get us as far as arming ourselves with a kitchen utensil and standing in a line at the couch or bed, or whichever piece of furniture housed the impaled animal.

'It can't hurt you!' my father would urge from the sidelines. 'Just hook the spatula behind it and drag it towards you.'

One by one, we would run screaming from the room, having barely got a mouse hair on our happy pants.

Soon after Franny was born a family of rats moved into my and Sam's bedroom wall. We were so busy through the night we barely noticed our new housemates. Any nocturnal scratches and scuttles were chalked up to a transient possum or toddler creeping towards the bassinet with a shovel.

'Please I can hit it with a stick, Mum?' Dee Dee asked about three weeks after Franny was born. She had just returned from the garden after carefully selecting her weapon.

'I won't let you do that. I noticed you said "please", though. Well done for using your manners.'

Franny fed every two hours and Dee Dee's sleep regressed due to the unfamiliar baby noise. Every day became the morning after. Sam or I would wake up groggily on the floor of the kids' room or the laundry, having no memory of how we got there. Franny cried unless she was being held or fed so I learned to sleep while doing both, usually for no longer than a couple of hours at a stretch. She would settle to sleep in her bassinet just as the sun and Dee Dee were rising. Cracks of light through the blinds would reveal the bottles, wet towels and soiled baby miscellanea strewn throughout the house, just as Dee Dee would wake and toddle through the carnage, expecting breakfast.

The first six months with a toddler and a baby are physical and psychological torture. After Franny's arrival, it became unclear to me how my mother managed to survive it on her own. She had double the kids and half the support. Her torture was quadruple the severity of mine. Octuple if you count the fact that we were all in cloth nappies. Even in the few years before my father left, he didn't parent. When he came home he expected sleeping children, a meal and a clean house. It was the 1980s and he travelled regularly for work. Their roles were very different and clearly defined. My mother spent her days working a factory line of children and my father provided financially. Their hairstyles were also very different and clearly defined, my mother sporting moussed curls and my father a gelled ponytail.

In 2018 it seemed, at least in my house, all parents were created equally exhausted. From Monday to Friday, Sam worked in an office and I stayed home to keep the kids alive, but outside of business hours, our parenting responsibilities were divided 50/50.

'Where are all the dummies?' he asked one night around 3 a.m. I was breastfeeding in the dark in the living room and he was settling Dee Dee in our bed.

I said I thought there was one in the car.

He said okay.

As Sam went to pick through the rubble of Cruskits and chewed library books for a beacon of latex, a creature made its way along the floorboards under the couch where I was seated. I pulled my legs up to my chest and listened, the flow of my breast milk ceasing abruptly. Whatever was under there wasn't in a hurry. Its pace was moderate, but purposeful, like it was shopping for a gift. I could hear its tail dragging along the wood. The sound of the back door caused it to scurry away.

'Found one,' said Sam, holding a dummy.

'They're both asleep,' I whispered.

'Cool.'

'We have rats.'

'Oh no. Are you sure?'

'One was just under the couch. I think it's gone now.'

'I'll get some bait tomorrow.'

'Okay.'

'Okay.'

I detached Franny and carried her into our bed, where the four of us slept for two fitful hours, while a large family of rats went about their business in our walls.

With no prior experience with rodent infestations, we threw some rat bait under the porch and considered ours handled. Over the weeks that followed, we simply ignored the fact that the scratching was steadily getting more pronounced. With our daughters barely old enough to hold a spatula, let alone drag one under the house for a rat fight, we resorted to my mother's strategy: avoidance. Franny had started sleeping for longer stretches through the night, but the wake-ups continued due to the rats' rich nocturnal life.

'Do you think we should call an exterminator?' Sam asked one night, pounding his fist on the wall behind our bedhead.

'I read somewhere that makes them die in the walls and bring plagues of blowflies,' I groaned.

He got up to turn the hallway light on. We found the light through the cracks in the floorboards helped to keep them contained.

The turning point was the day I discovered a dead one in the cubbyhouse. The rat was larger than I expected, about the size of an AFL football. It was curled on its side on the floor in a patch of sunshine from the window, as if it were taking a siesta. Its grey hair reflected the light so that it looked almost silver. Paddington Bear, a stuffed panda and a plastic figurine horse were seated around the cubbyhouse table in uncomfortable silence. Before them was an arrangement of wooden teacups and cakes, which remained untouched.

I stifled a scream and ran inside.

'What happen, Mummy?' asked Dee Dee.

'It's okay. I just hurt my eyes!'

'I give it a kiss.'

I kneeled and closed my eyes, and she pressed her mouth to each of my eyelids.

'Mmmah!' she said.

It helped a little.

I placed two strips of masking tape on the cubbyhouse door and was struck with guilt that I was in a partnership when my mother hadn't been. Sam would soon return home from work and dispose of the rat. He wouldn't enjoy doing it, but would feel obligated to on a deep and primal level. With every dead rodent on the doorstep, my mother used up one of her precious neighbourly favours, of which there were a finite amount. And yet the calculation made sense. Dead rodents were a psychological battle for her, and she needed to preserve her strength.

Once, at the supermarket, a woman casually asked: 'Are they all from different fathers?'

'Actually, it was the same cunt,' said my mother, hand on hip.

We never met the people who lived next door. They looked the other way if they saw us. They were an older couple, upstanding members of the community, my mother told me recently. The woman had dedicated her life to raising money for disadvantaged children. When she got sick, my mother took her a plant. It was the first and only time they spoke.

'Hello, I'm Lesley,' said my mother. 'I live next door.'

'Yes,' said the woman after a moment or two. 'I . . . hear you.'

'I'm sure you hear quite a bit from us,' my mother laughed, flustered.

The woman said nothing.

'Anyway, I wanted to . . . I brought you this plant.' My mother extended a potted orchid wrapped in cellophane.

The woman's arms remained at her sides.

'It's silly, really.' She extended it further.

The cellophane crinkled against the woman's elbow.

'Thank you,' she said at last, placing her hands weakly either side of it.

My mother nodded at the closing door and returned to her side of the fence, breaking into a run when she reached the driveway.

'Bugger, bugger, bugger,' she muttered, recalling the bolognaise likely burning on the stove.

I called an extermination company. The woman on the other end of the line explained that a treatment was unlikely to leave dead rats in my walls or plagues of blowflies in my living room. The poison they used would cause death by dehydration, forcing the rodents to flee their nest in search of water.

'They end up in the sewer, mostly,' she said.

'Oh God.'

I peered out at the cubbyhouse, dull under the sunless sky.

'What time can you send someone out?' I asked, shutting the blinds.

At 3 p.m. sharp there was a knock at the door.

'I've found the culprit!' I said, flinging it open with Franny in my arms. 'It was a baby crawling in the walls!'

'Haohh,' replied the woman standing on my doorstep. 'The name's Gloria. I'm here about the rats.'

I wondered how many Glorias in the world had ever uttered that sentence, and concluded it could be no more than five.

'Great, come in!'

Gloria was slight of build with a tough-guy swagger to her walk. She wore a large grey polar fleece jumper, dark grey cargo pants and a black baseball cap, which sat atop a shock of long thick hair that had been pulled into a ponytail. Her eyebrows were thin and arched, lending her face a look of surprise, softening her a little. Underneath them were two small suspicious eyes. When she spoke, she tilted her chin upwards, like she was sizing me up for a fight.

'Seen any inside the house?' she asked.

'Just heard them.'

'Right-o.'

'Would any have died from the bait we put down a few weeks ago?'

'Not likely,' she said. 'You might have got one or two of 'em at the time, but they wise up pretty quick. They send their young out to test the bait—you know, to see if it's poison.'

'Wow, I didn't realise they were so intelligent.'

Gloria looked at me like I was wearing rat traps for earrings. 'Dunno if I'd call mothers murdering their young "intelligent".'

I nodded. Who was I to challenge a small but terrifying woman's rat vendetta?

'There's a dead one in the cubbyhouse. How would that have happened?'

She sniffed and swaggered ahead of me down the hall. 'Probably got injured in a fight. Couldn't make it home.'

Gloria got to work laying poison down the side of the house. I put Franny and Dee Dee down for their naps.

Twenty minutes later there was a loud knock at the door. I tiptoed down the hallway past the girls' room. Gloria was standing there with a portable EFTPOS machine.

'All done. That'll be two hundred and twenty dollars,' she said.

'Oh, um, can you send me an invoice?'

'Nope, you gotta pay now.'

'I wasn't aware of that. I'm sorry. I can't pay you right now.'

'If I don't get payment, my boss is gonna come down on me like a tonne of bricks. Then I'm gonna come down on you.'

Down on you, down on you, down on you, down on you. Her words dissolved into a brief, but electric, sexual fantasy. I saw the two of us standing in the kitchen, me watching her remove her chunky gold hoops and place them on the bench, uncertain if she was going to fuck me or fight me. The zip on her polar fleece would descend to reveal a navy singlet stretched across her slight, capable frame, her tool belt slung low on her narrow hips. She'd crack her knuckles and the sound would cause a jolt through my body that was almost painful, like an animal brushing its snout against an electric fence.

'How far would you go to protect your young?' she would ask.

'All the way,' I'd whisper.

Back in reality, Gloria was staring down the barrel of her chin, her head cocked slightly to one side. I licked my lips and assumed my mother's hand-on-hip battle stance.

'Why don't you get your boss on the phone. I'd be happy to speak to them on your behalf.'

'Yeah, right-o,' she said.

'And please keep your voice down. My kids are asleep ... and I'd do anything to keep them from waking.'

I accepted her phone and arranged a funds transfer with her bulldog boss.

Afterwards, I marched to the cubbyhouse with a shovel to deal with the rat myself. 'This one's for you, Mum,' I said aloud, kicking the door open like Indiana Jones.

The macabre tea party scene remained unchanged, frozen in time, only the rat no longer shimmered in a patch of sunlight. Its fur was muddy grey. I ran screaming into the house. It was 5 p.m. Witching hour. I needed to preserve my strength.

THE SLUG: PART II

I found an anger support group that met in the evenings in the countryside. I liked that it wasn't called Taming the Bull or Chain Your Dragon, or anything equally veiny with testosterone. It was simply called Anger Support, which I interpreted as a non-judgemental space where I could feel less alone. The drive there and back was another appealing aspect; it would be long and childless and filled with music of my own choosing. The website was simple, listing only the address, the home number of someone named Joan and a photograph of the community hall where the meeting took place. The building looked to be made of weatherboard that had been painted white some time ago. Densely planted dahlias and honeysuckle grew either side of a path to the entrance, to the right of which was a sturdy-trunked apple tree, its long branches outstretched and fruit gleaming with knowledge. I felt certain that within the building's walls, not pictured, would be the answer for which I'd been searching my entire life.

I planned to arrive with an hour to spare, which I intended to spend with a seasonal soup and toast points in a charming country pub. But an hour before the meeting I still had an hour of driving ahead of me, so I settled for Red Rooster alone in my car. It was peak hour, and I was reminded that large numbers of people existed beyond the 100-metre strip from my house to daycare. They were commuting from the city to their homes in the outer suburbs, mostly alone and, from what I could gather, seething with rage. Next to me at the lights, a man clenched his jaw behind the wheel of his ute as a child gleefully kicked the back of his chair. His dead-eyed stare suggested a frustrating day on the site and a slowly evaporating soul, though it was difficult to decipher through the heavy window tint. Here was someone in desperate need of a mystery meeting in the woods. *They have a judgement-free vibe on their website*, I wanted to shout through the window as he sped away. *And dahlias!*

Eventually, mine was the only car on a narrow road,

weaving through a forest of towering ghost gums, their thin white trunks reflecting what was left of the light. I held my breath for most of it, visions of the car breaking down, hiking for phone reception and death by hypothermia dancing in my head. I'd been working my way through a tub of party mix from the servo a few towns back, and the sugar in my system was like petrol for my racing heart. My podcast had dropped out sometime earlier, leaving me in a silent car with the realisation that what I was doing was a little unhinged. The woman had seemed perfectly nice when we spoke on the phone a couple of weeks earlier, but still. I could have just booked an appointment with the last therapist I saw. I'd probably have saved on the amount I was spending on petrol.

Lazy. Insincere. You should drive off the road.

Variations on the last thought were becoming more frequent. In the middle of the night, alone in the bathroom, I'd dared myself to say aloud that I would kill myself, as if verbalising it would somehow make it contractual. A very unwell part of me believed it would be an act of love. And that my children would be better off without me. I said it three times, like *Candyman,* then returned to the bedroom and went to sleep, alone in my cocoon.

I cited 'negative self-talk' as my reason for booking in with a new therapist. She suggested I talk to myself like I'd talk to a friend, as a way of curbing feelings of shame or failure that could likely trigger a rage episode. She was a mother of small children too, and made me feel like I was normal. I didn't tell anyone about the incident in the bathroom. And besides, after a while it only troubled me from a distance, like a draught coming from the back of the house.

It was dark when I reached the hall. I parked the car and watched a torchlight bounce across the grass towards me. The figure holding it stopped at my window and I made out the features of an old woman in a thick knitted beanie.

'Hi,' I said, opening my window a crack.

'Are you Ashe?' she asked.

'Yes. Did we speak on the phone?'

'We did. I'm Nelly. How do you find the Subaru?'

'It's great.' I got out and followed her along the shadowy path, to the right of which stood the apple tree, its branches gnarled and bare. 'I've got little kids, so it's perfect for us.'

Inside was a sports net and a moustached man in a high-vis singlet.

'Good evening, Ray,' said Nelly. 'This is Ashe.'

'G'day, love, are you here for volleyball?' he asked.

'Hi, um, I don't think so.'

'She's with us,' said Nelly, showing me into a small adjoining room.

A wooden table took up most of the space, its light brown colour yellowed slightly by the fluorescent lights. Seated at it were two women who looked to be in their eighties. There was a faded image of a floral arrangement framed on the wall. In the corner was a chalkboard with the words 'Go easy' written in cursive, and underneath it 'Lend a hand'. A split system noisily filled the room with warmish air.

'This is Ashe,' said Nelly. 'Ashe, this is Sylvia and Joan.'

'Hello,' I said.

'A pleasure to meet you, welcome,' said Joan. Her voice was low and faint and her shoulders curled slightly forwards. Her authority was evident in the stillness of her body, and by the way she didn't pause between 'you' and 'welcome'. Also by the way she ended her sentence there. She was Joan from the website. There wasn't a doubt in my mind.

I sat on the chair closest to the door.

'Hello,' said Sylvia out of one side of her mouth, jerking her head slightly over her shoulder on the same side. She had a bouffant white hairdo and was the size of two Joans. She wore knitted fingerless gloves, and her hands were interlaced on the table in front of her.

Nelly closed the door and took the seat next to mine.

'Welcome to Anger Support, everybody,' said Joan. 'The meeting is now in session.'

A man's yell and the slap of rubber echoed in the main hall, which sounded very far away now that the door was closed.

I shifted in my chair.

The first ten minutes of the session were dedicated to administration. Joan explained the structure of the meeting, which was to apply the words on the chalkboard to an instance in our lives. Nelly—who, it was revealed, was the treasurer of the group—reported that there was $103.86 in the bank account.

'You said to provide a report,' she said, shrugging. 'So that was my report!'

'Thank you, Nelly, thank you,' said Joan. 'Let's begin now. "Go easy" is something we like to say in this group as a reminder to be gentle with ourselves and others. Sylvia, would you like to share a moment where that's applied for you this past week.'

'Well, I've been ill, as you know,' said Sylvia, 'and it's made me irritable to the point of not being able to stand anyone. Then I get depressed because I've spent too much time alone.'

I nodded, resisting the urge to say, *Speak on it, queen.*

'So I've been trying to "go easy", but it hasn't been a particularly easy week.'

Joan twitched her head. She had a long, thin sac of skin that hung from her chin. In this moment, it ricocheted spectacularly against the wool of her jumper.

'How could Sylvia have applied the assignment to her situation, Nelly, thank you. Thank you.'

Joan's 'thank you' could mean either 'speak' or 'stop speaking', but either way, one felt compelled to do it quickly.

'I'm a bit of a loner myself,' said Nelly. 'So a week on my own sounds fine to me. But if I'm being drawn into an argument with a neighbour or family member, I've found a way to avoid it, or "go easy", is to say, "You might be right," when what I mean is, "You might be wrong."'

Nelly pressed her lips together, the full stop to her mic drop. It was a good suggestion. I intended to use it the next time someone advised me on anything parenting related. I enjoyed both its veneer of generosity and broiling undertones.

Nelly's outfit confirmed her loner status: camouflage cargo pants, knitted rollneck, beanie and two variations of polar fleece. She was dressed for the apocalypse. Her shoes were bulbous and looked both unthinkably sturdy and impossibly comfortable. They were difficult to decipher between black, brown and grey. The colour combination was so dull and flat it seemed to emit an audible thud. Independence gets bandied about as a sexy term when applied to women, and usually involves high-heeled shoes that click clack out of penthouse doors to start again on their own.

But without a pair of Nelly's multi-terrain clompers, the underappreciated woman in the story would only make it so far. Nelly's shoes were the epitome of freedom. They took my breath away.

She shared a story about rescuing worms in her garden, her example of 'Lend a hand'. She'd been doing it for a few days.

'You see them trying to escape the bottom of the garden where it's too wet, or struggling across the pavement in full view of the magpies. How hard they have to work to move when they're off the dirt. But I'll probably get sick of it soon.'

'Where do you take them?' I asked.

'Oh, just to higher ground.'

'Okay, back on track now, everybody,' said Joan. 'Ashe, if you'd like to share how "go easy" might apply to your week, if you're comfortable, thank you. Thank you.'

It was silent apart from the squeak of rubber on floorboards in the main hall and muffled, gruff laughter.

Don't tell them. Don't tell anyone. You do not deserve help.

I started to cry. Nelly passed me a tissue and stood behind my chair. She placed a warm bony hand on my upper back. She didn't move or say anything, just stood there, like there was no limit to how long she would do it. It was her stillness that got me, and the quiet in the room. It was softer than the tissue in my hands, which was remarkably soft. You'd need at least $103 in your bank account to keep you in that kind of paper. Tears spilled out of my eyes like bucket loads wrung up from the bottom of a well.

I turned to Nelly and thanked her and she sat down again.

'I haven't been too easy on myself lately,' I said. 'I get angry at my kids. Sometimes scary angry.'

'Yep,' said Sylvia, with a firm singular nod. She knew.

'Ashe,' said Joan, hunching slightly more towards me. Her jacket was around her shoulders. The stiffness of the fabric made it stand upright on the back of her neck, framing the sides of her face like a Medici collar. This, combined with her impressive neckwear and natural leadership, gave her the mood and energy of Elizabeth I incarnate. I was all ears. 'When those kids are screaming and throwing things, hell, even throwing up, I want you to put a hand on your middle, your core, right on your belly, the part of you that's you, that's peaceful, and say, "No fear. Free from fear."'

It was something she used to say to herself before every shift at the jail. Joan had been a prison guard for most of her working life. 'Free from fear' was how she lived, like a tiny, humpback surfer paddling into 50-foot waves.

There was a thump at the door before it burst open. It was Ray, red from the volleyball court. Bessy had twelve puppies, we'd be happy to know. Mum and pups were all doing well. Ladies love this stuff, was the implication. He puffed his chest out with pride.

'How lovely,' said Nelly.

'Thank you, Ray,' said Joan, with her first smile of the evening. 'If you care to join us, you're always welcome.'

'Hahaha!' he roared. 'Oh no thanks, ladies!'

'Okay, Ray, thank you,' said Joan. The words seemed to push him backwards, still red and smiling. 'Ray. Thank you.'

The door closed.

We stood slowly and put on our hats and jackets. Then we crowded into a circle in the corner by the door. Joan asked us to hold hands and thanked us for being there. Hers were cool and papery. Sylvia's were doughy and warm. I lied about how far I had to drive home, not wanting to spook them.

It had rained during the meeting. Snails inched their way up the exterior wall of the building—in search of what, exactly? Theories ranged from higher ground to sex and death. A colony of bats flew high overhead, barely perceptible against the night sky. Nelly looked up and smiled.

'Lovely little creatures,' she said.

'Thank you,' I said. 'For listening to me and everything.'

The road gleamed like a river through the trees.

'It's slippery out there now. Get home safe.' She squeezed my arm. Her torchlight bounced into the brisk night.

In the car I rested my face in my hands, readying myself for the drive. I flinched and jerked them onto my lap, suddenly aware of their capacity to inflict pain. I thought about the night in the bathroom. Whatever compelled me to make that deal was the same thing that warned me to move my hands. It was just its style. Malice masquerading as concern.

'Alright, you slimy bitch,' I whispered, readying my journal and pen. 'No more whispering in the shadows. You have my full attention.'

The thing emerged coyly at first, a line about the blank page being an accurate depiction of my personality, just an optical tentacle, but it was just getting started. It oozed its hateful goo onto the page with words so cutting and precise I could hardly breathe. I read and re-read the page in front of me, my initial anguish giving way to bewilderment. It was absurd how badly this thing wanted to destroy me. It was desperate to. What the hell was its problem? Why was it so obsessed with me? It was a cruel and twisted maniac with no business being near my heart and soul. I ripped the paper in two, then four, then eight and dropped the pieces in a puddle next to the car, to sink back into the ground where they belonged.

KIT

'Milk?'

Noreen would shake her head.

I'd place a scalding mug of Irish Breakfast on the desk in front of her. Meanwhile Dee Dee would be on the floor in the corner, quietly alphabetising the touch and feel books.

'So we've got Peggy the hopeless harlot and Violet the dwarfish bear. I tink you've made rather a compelling case for sticking with tradition. There's safety in a father's name. Normalcy.'

'Or the perception of it,' I'd say. 'I don't believe it was the case for my great grandmother Kit. Or her daughter, for that matter. So clever Dee Dee! Now try it by illustrator.'

Noreen would take her cup in both hands and lean back in her chair. 'Alright, out with it then. Who was she and why do I care?'

Kit and her sister Ada were born on a farm in Gippsland. When they were teenagers, they became pregnant to an unknown father. They gave birth in secrecy a few months apart. Kit had a girl she named Gwendoline and Ada had a boy who was the spitting image of his grandfather. They were raised as siblings, and believed their grandparents to be their parents, which may have been half true. The family took over a sheep station in the South Australian outback, where Gwen and her brother would have very unhappy childhoods.

Kit gave birth to nine children during her lifetime, four of whom would make it to adulthood, which was slightly below average for the time. Kit never liked to play favourites with her kids, especially when it came to the dead ones, but suspected Maureen had been an angel, if there was such a thing. She had Down syndrome, polio and it was the 1940s. She was six when she died. There was a framed photo of Maureen on the wall of my nanna's living room, a beaming girl in a baby doll dress with cast iron leg braces. It used to frighten me. My nanna was Gwen. The one from the story.

Gwen was pregnant with my mother when she discovered Kit was her mother. She'd requested a copy of her birth certificate ahead of her shotgun wedding to my grandfather. It arrived in the mail at Kit's place.

'You might want to sit down before you open that,' said Kit, likely whispered so as not to wake Sid, asleep after a long night in the mines.

Sid was a tall, dark, handsome coal miner who liked to keep his wife to himself. Kit stole gasps of freedom when she could, sneaking into the ladies' lounge for a shandy after the weekly shop, that kind of thing. There was love there too. Together they maintained a huge vegetable garden in the backyard, bursting with life. Gardens were for sustenance, but Kit grew roses in the front yard. The best rose garden in Moe, she would have you know.

Kit and Ada remained close throughout their lives. After their husbands died, they were free to enjoy themselves any way they liked. They joined the bowls club and played pokies with jars of five cent coins. They spent summers at the Manns Beach Motor Inn, keeping to their room mostly, passing the time with puzzles, beer and packets of Turf Unfiltered. Ada didn't find happiness like Kit, but they had each other, together to the end in love and secrets.

Dee Dee would have drifted to sleep by that stage and awoken with a start at the sound of Noreen blowing her nose, a loud singular honk into an embroidered handkerchief.

'What a Godforsaken story,' she'd say.

'Baby, we don't know the half of it.'

'Alright, enough.' Noreen would return the hankie to her bag and snap it shut. 'We've been here for donkey's years. It's high time you take Miss ... Mackenport off to bed.'

I'd thank her and carry my sleeping baby to the car, having gracefully opted to save my thoughts on imposed prefixes for our next appointment. On the way home, I'd pass two elderly women walking slowly along the footpath. They'd be holding hands and smoking, the orange glow from their cigarettes like torches lighting the way.

WHEN TO STOP HAVING CHILDREN

My period is late. I am going to Bali with my father, leaving Sam and the kids behind. I will be gone for five days and four nights, an obscene amount of 'me time'. Surely enough to get me through the following decade. At least, that's the idea. Dee Dee has given me her blessing on the condition that I return with my toenails painted blue. Franny is on high alert. She has been running in and out of the bedroom while I pack, like an animal sensing a storm.

My suitcase contains four pairs of period-proof underwear, one moon cup and pads big enough to absorb a two-litre carton of orange juice. Before having children, my period was reasonably low maintenance, requiring only a dose of Panadol and a few tampons no larger than Tic Tacs. I could be a little moody the week before—some might argue violently unhinged (potato-potahto)—but for the most part it came and went with minimal fuss. Now it rendered me house-bound, expelling blood from my body like a vampire with food poisoning. I bleed like a person who has been reset to drain themselves of all resources, but even still, the arrival of my period never fails to wash me with a deep sense of relief.

It is wishful packing, a vision board for an empty womb. I know what happens to parents of three. I see them in the mornings, staring glassy-eyed through shop windows long before they open, a kid strapped to their chest and one to each leg, humming Freddy Krueger's nursery rhyme. In exchange for a third child, they sacrificed their last remaining shred of free will, yet the hope that they will get it back still remains. Therein lies the special brand of torture experienced by the parent of three. They are a prisoner with ocean views. This dangling carrot of hope can be lobbed off with the addition of a fourth child, and a fifth and sixth, if the person so desires. The final number makes little difference to anyone except their children in the future, when the population of our burning planet is divided into food and water scavengers. I imagine modern-day parents of four or more are forced into a state of monk-like acceptance, given that their life as an individual has been cancelled for the foreseeable future.

I was sure I didn't want more kids until Sam offered to get a vasectomy. I'd spoken to my doctor about it previously, and discovered that vasectomy patients were advised to undergo the procedure with the intent of permanently shutting down their fertility. They were reversible in some cases, but not in others. As she spoke, I pictured a darkened orphanage of unclaimed children tucked away in Sam's scrotum, their cries muffled by the boarded-up windows and howling blood vessels.

My father has eight children, two of them under five, a girl and a boy. Aunt and Uncle Baby. He is 63 and married to a woman who is a few years older than me. He doesn't plan on getting a vasectomy anytime soon.

The morning sky is coloured rose. My father is smoking a cigarette and leaning against the bonnet of his car, the eternal bad boy, still just beautiful enough to pull it off. He looks like Rod Stewart twenty years ago, post-second marriage, but pre-third. Same hair and nose. He's wearing aviator sunglasses with prescription lenses, like always.

'Yia sou, duck,' he says, in his own special language of pidgin English and Greek. He grew up in a suburb with a large Greek population, but no one's sure where it comes from beyond that.

'Yia sou, Dad.'

He puts my suitcase in the boot.

'I'm taking my daughter on a break,' he explains at the check-in desk, where a woman is studying the matching surname on our passports. 'She has two babies at home and needs a bit of R and R.'

He is pitching for better seats and at the same time clarifying that we are not husband and wife. He is also clarifying that our relationship needs clarifying despite our 30-year age difference.

'Ohhhhhhh!' says the woman. 'How great is your dad? I only have one baby at home and I'm so exhausted. I need ten trips to Bali.'

'They should sell them in a ten-pack for mums,' he says. 'The "me time" special.'

Some more banter ensues and we are awarded a row to ourselves with extra leg room.

We order coffee and sit at a table overlooking the tarmac. My father rests a spoon across the top of his long macchiato and pours sugar onto it from a sachet, allowing the weight of the sugar to sink the spoon into his coffee before stirring. I've watched him perform this ritual at least a hundred times. I add sugar to my coffee in precisely the same way. A toasted cheese sandwich arrives on floppy white bread, filled with a bright yellow soupy substance, which, if the smell is anything to go by, is the product of steeping cheese with arse. My father hasn't looked up from his newspaper in minutes, and there isn't a crying baby to soothe or nose to wipe as far as the eye can see. My focus is a sweating ball of food-like substance that has been moulded into the shape of a sandwich. That and the fear that the sandwich is just a sandwich, and my hyper-sensory experience is a sign of early pregnancy. I look hopefully around for a rogue toddler I might rescue from the jaws of an escalator, and, failing that, scan the floor for a dummy requiring sterilisation in a cup of boiling water sourced from a fast-food outlet in the manner of a contestant on *The Amazing Race*, but I find not a one.

I text Sam for an update. Dee Dee had a nightmare and was still asleep when I left. It was 7 a.m., and in all likelihood she would have been in complete distress waking up to me not being there.

Me: *Is she okay?*
Sam: *Sweet as a nut*

He sends a picture of her grinning over a bowl of cereal. He needs me to believe in his capability to parent without me, so much so that he is willing to curb-stomp my heart via text.

Me: *x*

I commend myself on my composure in the face of Sam's emotional barbarity.

On the plane, we sit behind a family of five: two parents, a one-year-old and two kids who look to be around five and seven. The parents are in the aisle seats, taking turns to bounce the one-year-old on their knee. In the middle are the two older children, watching complimentary Disney movies from chairs that cost $600 a piece.

'Ask Daddy to get you some water,' says the mother. 'I've got my hands full holding your brother right now.'

The parents communicate almost exclusively through the children for the duration of the flight, which strikes me as a symptom merely of the physical distance between them rather than an emotional one. Maybe it's a symptom of both.

'Did you plan the third one?' I want to hiss in her ear from between the seats. 'Are you okay? Would you describe yourself as a prisoner with ocean views?'

Later in the flight, I stare meaningfully at her while waiting to go to the toilet, but her eyes are fixed straight ahead. Both she and her partner are bathed in the delicate blue light of the screen above them. He is holding the now-sleeping one-year-old while the other two children lie sprawled across either parent, who would sooner watch several hours of flight information than risk waking one of their kids while reaching for the remote.

At Denpasar airport, the customs line is already 100 metres long. My father tilts his head towards the special circumstances line, consisting of the family of five and an elderly person in a wheelchair.

'That's the perk of travelling with kids,' he says. 'Can you fake a limp or something?'

'Dad, are you serious?'

He looks longingly at the shorter line, mentally calculating the risk of faking a limp versus the reward. Meanwhile, another flight of people joins the back of our line and we become buried in the middle.

'We've missed the window now,' he says.

I breathe a small sigh of relief. 'And look how many people are behind us!'

He glances over his shoulder. 'Hey,' he says, elbowing me in the side. 'They aspire to be us.'

My father is a master of being present, but not in the way they encourage at yoga. He wants the thing that he wants, and has little to no concept of consequence. He is absolutely present in his moments of wanting, as if nothing exists either side of them. It's the reason he continues to smoke a pack a day despite the advice of his team of cardiologists.

We arrive at the villa and I put my bag in my room. The windows drip with condensation from the air conditioner. I lie face down on the king-size bed, my head at the foot of a mountain of carefully stacked throw pillows, and cry tears of relief, the volume of which strikes me as alarmingly disproportionate to my level of hydration.

I change into my bathers and go outside to the pool, where my father is lying on his back on the stone tiles wearing black speedos. His feet are in the water and both his arms are outstretched, welcoming the midday Indonesian sun. In one hand, smoke from his unfiltered rollie curls into the humid air. This is the sunbaking moment. I get a can of Coke from the fridge and ask if he wants one.

'No thanks, love,' he says, dragging deeply on his cigarette. 'My body is a temple.'

That evening, we walk single file through Seminyak. Vehicles jostle within arm's reach of the narrow footpath, which disappears at random. Crossing a main intersection, my father grabs my hand, leading the way across eight lanes of traffic. An unprecedented stream of cars and scooters round the corner and we break into a jog, my father holding out his free hand while I cover my belly with mine.

It's dark when we get to the restaurant, a family barbecue place with a thatched roof and heavy wooden tables. Photos of glistening tourists deck the walls. Most of the tables are occupied by parents and young children with special holiday bedtimes. Two have fallen asleep at the table beside us. Their arms are folded neatly above their heads. A woman in a floral maxi dress squeezes past us with a new baby flopped over her shoulder. My left ovary calls my right to coo into her fallopian phone.

'When are you getting a vasectomy?' I ask my father after we order, having run out of small talk some hours prior.

'As soon as they have an appointment ... is what I tell my wife.'

'Do you actually want more kids?'

He lights a cigarette. 'No, but ask me again tomorrow.'

He loves being a father and adores each of his children individually—but, I imagine, especially as a group, when the eight of us can act as a force field of youth and vitality around him.

Over dinner, we talk about his daughter, who is having trouble making friends at school. He shares how he taught her 'conversation starters' like, 'What's your favourite colour?' and 'I love your pencil case! Where did you get it?' He's a better parent now, he wants me to know, which he is. No question.

That night, I lie awake mentally baby-proofing the villa. I worry most for hypothetical Franny, who embodies the drive of the Terminator and the co-ordination of Bambi on ice. The steps descending from the living room to the unfenced pool would be my main concern, followed by the decorative rock gardens concealed in soft beds of tropical greenery. The smoking mosquito coils beneath the furniture would be just out of reach of searching hands, but the potential for malaria would be everywhere. Finally, I drift into a sequence of light stress dreams about punctured pool floaties and pram wheels caught in pavement cracks.

'Here you are,' says my father the following morning, pushing an Australian newspaper across the table.

I'd woken up early and waited outside a nearby cafe while the staff set up the furniture, figuring my holiday-induced insomnia might be an opportunity to get some work done. So far, I had achieved scrolling through several hundred photos of the kids.

'This is what you should be writing,' he says, pointing to a personal essay submited by a reader. 'You could call it "Travels with My Father".'

I close my laptop and read it while he continues to pen my entry.

'*When he took my hand across the busy road, I was transported back to childhood, to being a little girl again . . .*'

'Dad, this person's teenager died. We're going to need a better story than that.'

'I don't know—say I used to burn you with cigarettes or something!'

A waitress asks him if he would like to order, and he says he'll have coffee outside and will eat anything 'but that', gesturing to my plate.

He leaves me with the newspaper and my regretful order of hard-boiled garden clippings. I re-read the essay. It was a freak accident on a family sailing trip. The unmentionable happened, but hardly the unthinkable. 'What if' and the infinite combination of words to complete the sentence played on a low frequency in my mind at all times. The submission had been written by the mother after some healing had occurred. She wrote about the smell of dried basil in the boat's galley kitchen and in her pantry at home after years had gone by. Underneath the flowery imagery was an unpatterned message of hope: You'll be okay someday, kind of.

What if my children continued their dumb health lottery luck? What if they happened to stay on the parts of the road where the dangerous drivers were not? What if they made it through their school years and the idiocy of their twenties? What if they made it all the way to their timely deaths?

My last trip to the op shop had been a tearful one, involving a garbage bag of knitted booties and squeaky baby toys. As Dee Dee progressed from baby to toddler, we had carefully stored away her outgrown items in anticipation of her sibling. When Franny grew out of them, I kept them all the same, but not for practical reasons or even sentimental ones. I couldn't shake the feeling that I was turning my back on my unborn children, the equivalent of siblings three to eight in my family.

I donated breast milk to another compulsive breeder after Franny was born.

'I just couldn't imagine my life without any of my kids,' she said, breathless and bursting with a full-term pregnancy.

'How many do you have?' I asked.

'Four.' She cradled the base of her belly. 'Soon to be five. After my first child, I realised that he was *essential* to my existence, and then my second child came along and *she* was essential. Then I had my third . . .'

'Same thing?' I asked, noting her grip on the small medical-grade ice box she'd brought to transport the milk.

'Exactly! And now I can't stop thinking about all the children I'm *not* having, you know?'

'Yeah,' I said, and considered thawing some milk and throwing it in her face to break the craze. She was caught on a loop, chasing a meaningful existence like a dog chasing its tail. On one level, I admired her spirit.

It's our last night in Bali and my period still hasn't arrived. My father and I are having dinner at a restaurant that specialises in margaritas, a fact we are unaware of until someone orders one and the female wait staff dance in formation to Taylor Swift's 'Shake It Off'.

'Jesus Christ,' says my father, glancing briefly at the dancers and witheringly at the diner responsible.

I haven't seen him since this morning. He seems tired and detached. I try not to take it personally. The restaurant opens to the busy footpath and the air is coated with stupefying heat.

'Since we've been "sharing" these past few days,' he says, putting air quotes around the word 'sharing' in rejection of a hokey, therapy-esque term, a way to protect himself, 'I'm going to "share" something with you now.'

'What are you saying?' I dab my sweat moustache with a paper napkin.

'I've had an angina episode today.'

'What?'

'A heart thing.'

'Shake It Off' blares again through the speakers for a few words of the chorus then stops abruptly, as if someone has pulled the plug. The chorus line of waitresses hold their shakers high in the air.

'Dad, are you okay?'

'I feel good now. I found two pills in the bottom of my bag, so I've taken one and I have one more if I need it.'

'What pills?'

The song blares loudly again, this time to completion, at which point one of the dancers appears panting at our table.

'If . . . you . . . would like . . . a dance . . . you . . . must order . . . a special margarita.'

We thank her and my father compliments her on her hair ribbons.

'What pills?' I ask again.

'Nitroglycerin. You know in the movies when a guy's dying from a heart attack and he says, *Get . . . my . . . pills*?' He puts his hands to his throat and mimes a movie death.

'Don't you need more than one?'

'Ideally yes. I have my prescription from home, which is lucky. We can go to a chemist after dinner and see if they'll fill it for me.'

I say okay, and eat all the bacon in our shared Caesar salad.

Outside the restaurant I am googling 'chemist near me' while my father speaks to some locals on scooters, momentarily disappearing into the shadows.

'There's a chemist a hundred metres that way,' I say when he reappears. 'What did those guys say?'

'Those guys? Nothing, they just sold me Valium. For the plane.'

'Dad.' The memory of his last heart attack is right

there. His outline moving in slow motion down the driveway in bare feet. Walking to show us we didn't need to worry. Flummoxed paramedics following him with the empty stretcher.

We walk past a large bright convenience store.

'Let's go in here,' he says.

'Is there a chemist in there?'

'Not sure, love.'

He buys rolling tobacco for himself and an assortment of rubber sea creatures for his four-year-old son. 'A diving game,' he decides aloud.

'Special Balinese picnic rug for Livi,' he says, tugging a sarong for his five-year-old from a pile on display.

This is the shopping moment. I look dumbly around for the nitroglycerin section while he breezes the aisles for last-minute magical gifts. Satisfied with his purchases, he pays and lights a cigarette while we wait for our car to the airport.

The chemist trail has gone cold. I study the blur of shopfronts through the car window regardless. There's bound to be one at the airport, my father had said. *Worst-case scenario*. He discusses the area's new nightclub with the driver and how it's impacting local businesses.

I sit quietly in the back seat wording and rewording my plea, an appeal to my father's paternal instinct, positioning him getting medical attention as a way of sparing me a lifetime of blame should he die on the plane—delivered in the least dramatic way, but with enough passion for him to hear it. Restrained but pained, a level voice, a sheen of tears.

The airport is near empty, like a big-budget film set on lunch. My father nods politely at my suggestion that I run ahead to look for a chemist. There isn't one, I report back, heart racing, abdomen cramping. He says he's feeling great and we should check in. The heart scare storyline is a distant memory, as relevant as the name of a pirated movie he once owned on DVD.

At the check-in desk, he turns to me, patting the pockets of his jacket. 'But where is . . .'

Oh God. The last pill. He's lost it.

'My passport. Ah, here it is.'

We sit on plastic chairs by the gate, side by side, closer than we have been for the duration of the holiday. He says he read one of my blogs, and asks why I didn't tell him I had postnatal depression. He wishes I did.

'Just a phone call, that's it,' he says.

I am watching a woman kneeling on the carpet in a burgundy velour tracksuit. She is roughly brushing her head of long, thick hair, like she's been wrestling with it her whole life.

'It wasn't that easy, Dad. I didn't think I deserved help.'

'It must be because of social media. All the comparison. It can't be healthy.'

'Maybe . . .' I turn to face him. He continues facing forwards. He too is watching the girl with the hair. I address his ear and the whiskers on his cheek. 'Dad, do you love yourself?'

He is quiet for a moment.

'I don't know too much about that, I'll admit. But I try to be thankful for my life. That's it. Do you?'

It was an offer, the first of its kind. I didn't love myself for a long time. I'd believed it was because of him, the only man to ever break my heart. The one who took my sisters and I for walks on the beach during storms, bundled in coats, with a Thermos of hot chocolate in the pocket of his. The one whose love was dangerous in that it could become invisible. The one sitting here next to me.

I say I'm working on it.

Ponytail in place, the woman zips her brush away in her bag and falls back exhausted against the wall.

On the plane, I take half a Valium and curl up in a row to myself. My father lies across the one in front, his mess of sand-coloured hair protruding into the aisle. My eyes close for a moment then open to the reassuring sight. I decide not to blame myself if he dies, out of love for both of us, asleep together on separate rows, hurtling through the sky.

I wake up groggily a few hours later to a breakfast tray. My father has ordered on my behalf, and arranged my coffee with a serviette he has folded just so. He would discover upon seeing his specialist that it was a case of extreme reflux, which had presented as the early signs of a heart attack. But he'd worry about all that later. This was the breakfast moment.

I go to the restroom just before we land. I discover the arrival of my period and waves of grief and relief wash over me.

It's 7 a.m. when I get home. The sound of my key in the lock triggers a stampede down the hallway and I crouch to receive them, the three of us falling backwards onto the floor. Sleep has spun their hair into nests on the crowns of their heads. They smell like milk and muesli. 'Mum, Mum, Mum,' they're saying. This is the toddler moment. And I'm here, here, here.

Ashe Davenport is a Melbourne-based author and family columnist for The Design Files. Her debut book began as a personal blog called *Sad Pregnant Lady*, which would become *Sad Mum Lady*. These days she's a mother of two, and a somewhat happier person.